DANCING IN THE CAVE OF THE DRAGON

Adventures in the Wonderland of Sales

From Sales Satirist
Richard Plinke

Dragon Press
2019

Richard Plinke is an
Author, Speaker, and Trainer.

His other books are:

From the Jaws of the Dragon:
Sales Tales and Other Marginally Related Stuff

More Droppings from the Dragon:
A Hitchhiker's Guide to Sales

For more information, please visit
www.howtoselltheplague.com

for Howie

I hope this one finally fixes that
wobble on your kitchen table.

Risk

a situation involving exposure to danger

My mission in life is not merely to survive, but to thrive; and to do so with some passion, some compassion, some humor, and some style.
~ **Maya Angelou**

If you are never scared, embarrassed or hurt, it means you never take chances.
~ **Julia Sorel**

Do you want to be safe and good, or do you want to take a chance and be great?
~ **Jimmy Johnson**

The only safe thing is to take a chance.
~ **Mike Nichols**

Security is mostly a superstition. Life is either a daring adventure or nothing.
~ **Helen Keller**

Only those who will risk going too far can possibly find out how far it is possible to go.
~ **T.S. Eliot**

Living at risk is jumping off the cliff and building your wings on the way down.
~ **Ray Bradbury**

Do not fear mistakes. There are none.
~ **Miles Davis**

Do one thing every day that scares you.
~ **Eleanor Roosevelt**

Twenty years from now you will be more disappointed by the things you didn't do than by the ones you did. So throw off the bowlines, sail away from the safe harbor, catch the trade winds in your sails. Explore. Dream. Discover.
~ **Mark Twain**

If you risk nothing, then you risk everything.
~ **Geena Davis**

Opportunity dances with those on the dance floor.
~ **Anonymous**

Contents

1

Introduction

Writing this book has been a challenge. I started it in 2015, intending to publish it in 2017. I'm a freak for symmetry: My first book came out in 2013, my second in 2015, and 2017 fit Nicely-Nicely-Johnson into that order and kept my world spinning safely on its axis. Until...

September 2015: I was really digging into the new book when I was diagnosed with tongue cancer. I was so distressed over the news that they had to rush me to the hospital two weeks later with a blockage in one of my main arteries. Apparently, stress can cause what they call an eruption of plaque that moves through your arteries until all the fragments meet up and cause a blockage. They told me my other arteries were pristine (loved that one), put in a stent and sent me on my way. Soon after, they excised the cancer from my tongue, a swell operation that left me eating the most putrid, foul-tasting crap all through the Christmas holiday.

Fun times.

So, by spring, I'm feeling better and writing again when out of nowhere, wham! I'm back in my doctor's office looking at a PET scan of the lymph nodes in my neck. My doctor points to one with a small black dot and tells me the chances of it not being cancer are less than zero.

A screaming comes across the sky.

How do you even equate "less than zero?"

So, back in for more surgery, where they removed 60 lymph nodes and rearranged the symmetry of my face. Fortunately, most of the damage blends in well with my aged, craggy countenance, so instead of resembling Elephant Man, I look more like a football.

So, I'm recovering nicely-nicely after they removed the drainage tubes from my neck and chest that made me look like something out of the Borg Collective, and I'm starting to write again when wham! They decide I need radiation treatment. Well, I didn't really need radiation treatment because they got everything and I was clean, but it would be the prudent thing to do. For whom? To help the hospital pay for the radiation machine?

So, six weeks (seven if you want to count the fitting process), five treatments a week, bolted down to a stainless steel gurney in a mask and mouthpiece that make it hard to breathe and impossible to move and every time they clamp down the damn thing, my nose starts itching.

So, I'm into my fourth week and I start to blister, ending up with second-degree burns on my shoulder.

So, I'm finished radiation (finally), and I get shingles.

So, I'm over the shingles and I get walking pneumonia.

So, I'm over walking pneumonia and I get every virus and bacterial infection I can find because my immune system has been shot to hell. They tell me not to worry; it's temporary. Just like my dry mouth. Just like my loss of taste. Just like the pain in my neck. Just like the debilitating pain in my shoulder from nerve damage, for which I now get to experience months of therapy.

Oh joy!

But wait. There's more.

Winston Churchill said, "If you're going through hell, keep going."

Like I had a choice.

So, I go to the dentist for a checkup, and it ain't nicely-nicely. Between the dryness in my mouth and the powerful radiation poisoning, I have cavities for the first time in decades, need a few caps and an implant. But first they have to pull the dying tooth, a big deal after radiation as they fear the bone may be too weak to handle the intrusion.

So, I end up in a hyperbaric oxygen tank to help strengthen the jaw bones — 20 treatments, five days a week, then they pull the tooth, then back in for 10 more treatments. Six weeks in an airtight, sealed decompression chamber for two hours a day. They tell me they have to sedate many people. I understand but can handle it, although even after radiation, myriad PET scans and MRIs, it's still unnerving, especially because I know that a slight spark can blow the whole thing up — with me in it!

So, it's getting on in 2018 by now and I'm starting to write again, and then wham! A young man late for work rams into the back of my car at 60 miles an hour while I'm stopped in traffic. Back in the ambulance, back in the hospital, back in therapy for a severe concussion and extensive neck/shoulder damage.

So, it's 2019 and I'm slowly recovering from the accident and beginning to be able to do some work at the computer when wham! — I have knee replacement surgery. The accident had aggravated the knee and considerably hastened the necessity of the surgery.

So, back in therapy for my knee and still in therapy for the concussion and neck/shoulder problems and I'm about sick to death of all this!

So, I'm on the mend and feeling better and, obviously, writing again as I punch out these last few words, finally finishing a book I've lived with through so much: Such as the death of four important people in my life. It started right after my first surgery on February 7, 2016, when Dick Swoboda died. I met Dick in a bar in Chicago ... on purpose. We had set up the meeting in advance to talk business and quickly discovered we were kindred spirits.

Next came (or should I say went) Howie Gelbert, who died on January 19, 2017, not too long after my second surgery. Howie and I knew each other only six years, but because of our remarkable similarities in histories and experiences, coupled with the comfortable familiarity of shared irreverence toward the supercilious and doltish, it was as if we had been friends our entire lives. Howie was a good man with a big heart; a true mensch. He had an uncanny knack for collecting people, and the marvelous gift of spreading happiness. No loss has ever affected me the way Howie's has; his death left a hole in my life that can never be filled, except by his stupid jokes replaying in my mind over and over again, just like Howie used to tell them: over and over again.

"D'ya hear the one about the frog ... ?"

This book is dedicated to Howie.

Not too long after that, on May 31, 2017, my old friend and mentor, Ned Ross, passed away after a long and courageous battle with cancer. I have so many great memories of Ned, and learned so much from him. He was always supportive and vital to my success.

Finally, on August 11, 2017, Bob Coward, one of the sweetest men I've ever known, left us. Bob was a good friend who, years earlier, had helped me through one of the darkest periods of my life. All four of these men meant a great deal to me and helped me in more ways than they ever knew. After Bob died, I posted the following on Facebook:

"I've had a hard time dealing with *time's winged chariot hurrying near,* and all these transitions have suffused me in a dull pallor of melancholy. But I've grown weary of feeling sorry for myself and am instead going to take satisfaction in having known these good men who gave me something more valuable than silver or gold: They made me feel important."

Though nothing can bring back the hour
Of splendor in the grass, of glory in the flower;
We will grieve not, rather find
Strength in what remains behind.

So I beat on, boat against the current, borne forward into the future (with compliments to F. Scott Fitzgerald), writing again and finishing the last few words of this *long and winding road*. While all the king's horses and all the king's men were stitching me back together again, I'd been working diligently (if somewhat erratically) to stitch together these meager offerings for your reading pleasure (or not — who am I to say?). Which is why I give you this brief history of my adventures in the wonderland of restorative amelioration: Because of the long duration it took to create this work, some of the pieces may seem a wee bit disjointed. Now, to those of you not visiting my rodeo for the first time, you're probably saying to yourselves, "So what else is new?"

Fine.

But in this case, because of the lapse of time, I feel the need to explain a few of the chapters that may seem dated. That said, please keep in mind that the current events I write about generally are vehicles to deliver my messages, and because of that, I think they still hold up, and maybe they're even a bit quaint at this point.

1. "Vote for Me, I'll Set You Free:" This one's from the 2016 presidential primary races. Not only do I stand behind everything I wrote in the piece, but it was a pretty good prognostication. The topic is one of my favorites.

2. "Everywhere There's Lots of Piggies:" I wrote about TARP in this one. TARP stands for Troubled Asset Relief Program, instituted by the federal government in 2008 to help financial institutions, like turning on the lights for the burglars.

3. "White Noise:" This one is about the death of Prince and the rise of Donald Trump. Cool stuff! Also, a blatant pitch for sales training.

4. "Rhinoceros? Imposerous!:" Here we have rhinoceri running wild through Allentown, Pennsylvania. No, not really; not like lions and tigers and bears, oh my! And yes, I know I've used that line before ("Light Up Your Face with Gladness" in *From the Jaws of the Dragon*), but if you know anything about me, you know I have a reckless proclivity for using favorite quotes and phrases *ad nauseum* — what can I say? Deal with it! Anyway, I love this piece, but it uses TV commercials that have

been off the air for a couple of years. I hope you still recognize them. I also reference the killing of Cecil the lion in 2015. If you don't remember that sad tale, you can read about it on the internet.

5. "All the Wrong Junk in All the Wrong Places:" Here we have Charlie Sheen in an interview with Matt Lauer, trying to be humble and sincere — another one of my favorite topics. There is plenty of irony in this one as Lauer questions Sheen about his sexual indiscretions, before Lauer's own inappropriate behavior was made public and he lost his job. I thought about rewriting it, but the piece isn't about sexual transgressions; it's about body language, so I left it to stand on its own merits.

6. "Tattoos of Memories and Dead Skin on Trial:" I wrote this one, featuring Tide Pods, only a year ago, but things come and go so quickly around here.

7. "Total Eclipse of the Brain:" Another one of my favorites. It's about the 2017 eclipse; I hope the joke about Chris Christie still works.

And I hope the rest of the book stands up well and reads nicely-nicely. As with my other books, many of the chapters in this one are from columns I wrote for business publications, but a good bit of the material is new, written in the last few months, enthused by my good fortune of having worked with five incredibly gifted young people this past summer at Lehigh University. I mentored them at the Iacocca Institute's Global Village, an intensive, five-week leadership experience that helps build cross-cultural leadership, professional, business and entrepreneurial skills while preparing the villagers to thrive in a global community. Cristina Giza from Moldova, Ganna Lachykhina from Ukraine, Arturo Perrotta from Italy, Brett Seidner from the United States and Azamat Tarasbaev from Kazakhstan lifted my spirits and helped me across the finish line. They were truly inspirational; not to mention they renewed my hope in our future on this decomposing ball of volcanic residue.

And speaking of balm for the soul, I was on a family vacation at the beach this summer when one of my progeny — a 9-year-old boy with a keen perspective named Preston — had undertaken the arduous task of trying to open a plastic box of cookies. After struggling for a while with the satanic container, he handed it to an adult and asked him to open it. As the adult wrestled with the over-engineered packaging, he teased Preston: "So what, you want one of these cookies?"

Without losing a beat and in a calm and deliberate voice, Preston answered, "No. I want them all."

Proud I was.

Thanks for sticking with me — hope you get all the cookies.

Allentown, Pennsylvania
August 18, 2019

2

Prologue

Yo! How you doin'? Thanks for coming back, or if you're a first-time traveler, welcome aboard. Today's light topic is the meaning of life, so let's jump right in.

Lots of lip service floating around out there about doing the right thing. Everybody with 15 minutes of fame has chimed in, and with all that advice and all those clever memes coming at us, you'd think we'd be in better shape. But alas, *talking* about doing the right thing and *doing* the right thing are two different matters. And to make those matters worse, one person's ceiling is another person's floor. In other words, the right thing is not a universally agreed-upon concept — what's right for one may not be (and in today's polarized world, usually isn't) right for the other.

So, my question is: What is the right thing? That's really an age-old mystery that mankind has struggled with for eons, ever since Keith Richards crawled out of the sea and grew fingers. While it may be difficult to find an absolute for doing the right thing, doing the wrong thing is a much easier proposition. If I didn't know that before, I learned it in spades when my assistant gave me a book for Christmas titled *The History of the World in Bite-Sized Chunks,* by Emma Marriott. The small tome took me through a complete chronicle of the human race from the beginning of recorded civilization, and the central theme was mainly about killing and enslaving each other. These are the most prominent consistencies I found throughout our development and in all different cultures. And remarkably, we don't appear even close to being done with them.

You may think we've advanced, but when you look at our history from 30,000 feet, it's pretty much the same story, only we've gotten better at it. Whereas we no longer enslave folks to build our pyramids or pick our cotton, we now subjugate them to vote for us. Furthermore, we can't cure the common cold or replace the internal combustion engine, but we can kill the crap out of one another in all multitudinously ingenious manner. We really are masters of the universe when it comes to mistreating our fellow opposable-digited hominids.

And it's that time-honored tradition of brutality, mayhem and destruction upon which we've built our enlightened civilization, a civilization that has given us a true understating of the trickle-down theory — we're all much better at doing the wrong thing than the right thing because doing the wrong thing has been handed down from generation to generation as doing the right thing. It may be hard to figure out what the right thing is when doing the wrong thing is celebrated and paraded down Main Street and disguised in so much subterfuge that it's hard to know what's up and what's down.

In the world of business, you're taught not to ask those kinds of prickly questions, like why are we a bunch of lying thieves? I found that out quickly when I went to work selling Yellow Pages advertising right out of college. "We don't need no stinking ethics" was the well-camouflaged battle cry of the avaricious rationalizers who could pick a pocket faster than a speeding sales pitch. This was not subtle stuff I'm talking about, either, but out-and-out fraud and larceny, and if you'd like to know more, it all will be in my book *How to Sell the Plague,* due out in 2020. (What a deceitful thing to do, eh?)

I can, however, tell you about some other cool debauchery and madness I was exposed to during my years in corporate America (if you're still interested; if you haven't thrown this book away after my shameless, yet smooth attempt at preselling and making more money — I told you this is about the meaning of life, didn't I?).

After leaving the Yellow Pages, I went to work in the out-of-home advertising industry. My first job was with 3M, the international conglomerate that had a billboard division. That division had sprung out of 3M's development of reflective tape, which was used on small, unilluminated highway signs around the country, usually in rural areas, advertising motels and restaurants and local insurance agents. They were built on wooden poles sometime during the Cretaceous Period, so many of them were covered in overgrowth or blocked by trees, and it was my job to figure out how to sell signs that nobody could see.

I complained to my pragmatic (read perfidious) boss about it and he bought me a chainsaw.

"To cut down the trees and brush?" I innocently inquired.

"To cut down the signs you can't sell," he scoffed, like I'd just shown up on the back of a rutabaga truck.

"Won't losing that inventory upset the company?" I innocently inquired.

"The company wants you to cut down those signs," he scoffed, like I'd just shown up on the back of a rutabaga truck.

So for the next year, I proceeded to cut down any sign I deemed unsellable, and in so doing, increased my occupancy levels dramatically. At the next annual meeting, the divisional VP complimented me on the fine job I had done in increasing the usage numbers, but he was dismayed at all the signs that had fallen down in the territory. "Once those signs are down, they can never be replaced because of strict permitting," he told me.

My boss, who was standing next to me, agreed. "It's an unfortunate loss to the company," he said, "but many of the poles out there are rotting away. It's too bad we couldn't repair them before they collapsed."

So much for innocent inquiries.

My next stop was with a large billboard company in Philadelphia, where my tutorial on lying and cheating (or business as usual) was accelerated with extreme prejudice. We had a general manager there who was ... how should I put this?

... a lying, cheating, reprobate, degenerate, scoundrel scumbag. He was no good to the core, which is why he did so well and got promoted to the highest position in the market.

We sold a program of billboards to a cigarette company that was launching a new product and wanted to blitz the market with a quick-hitting 30-day campaign. That campaign entailed using 16 large, 14-by-48-foot billboards. When the tobacco people placed the order, our market was sold out, but instead of telling the client the truth, that we had no room, the GM double-booked the business — he took their money even though we had no space for their ads. The client had requested proof-of-performance pictures of all the billboard sites, not an unusual demand, so at the end of the 30-day period, just before the pictures were due to the client, the GM had one billboard produced and sent it with a crew to go from location to location, hang the hand-painted display on each billboard frame, take its picture and then move it to the next site.

Nice work if you can get it, and you can get it if you try, as long as you're a lying, cheating, reprobate, degenerate, scoundrel scumbag.

There's more to that story, but I think I'll save it for *How to Sell the Plague*. Yeah, yeah, yeah — you didn't pay for an ongoing promotional teaser and all that rot. Pish posh!

From Philadelphia I went to Chicago to a larger billboard company, one I hoped would cleanse my soul and nourish my abused psyche.

Ha!

Those boys in Chicago made the GM in Philadelphia look like a piker. It didn't take long for me to discover that the whole real estate department — the folks responsible for leasing new billboard sites — was made up of a bunch of lying, cheating, reprobate, degenerate, scoundrel scumbags. One of their more interesting practices was to use the development of new locations to steal money from the company: If they came across a property that was undeveloped and relatively inexpensive as they were scouting out new sites for potential billboards, they would buy it and then negotiate a lease with themselves on behalf of the company — at an exorbitant rate, of course. As a result, the company was paying an average lease cost much higher than the market should have borne, and the real estate rogues were pocketing the extra loot. But since the regional VP and the other top brass were also lying, cheating, reprobate, degenerate, scoundrel scumbags, they turned a blind eye to the institutionalized corruption.

They had little choice. They were up to their eyeballs in the systemic larceny. We had a beautiful, elaborately decorated, well-stocked conference room that doubled as a libatious clubhouse for the Hole-in-the-Wall Gang. They justified it by saying its purpose was to entertain important clients, which I guessed happened when I wasn't in the building, and that was peculiar because I was usually in and out of the building five days a week, eight to 10 hours a day — I would have been there on Saturdays and/or Sundays, too, but on weekends it was locked up tighter than a frightened clam. Hey, maybe that's when they did their important client entertaining.

What they did do when they weren't entertaining said apocryphal important clients was drink. I learned quickly that if I needed anything done with the assistance of management, get it done in the morning, because once the clock struck 12, it was guzzle, guzzle time. By mid-afternoon on most days, the *modus operandi* was swaying and slurring to the beat of *I want to get drunk, I'm gonna make it real clear. I want one bourbon, one scotch and one beer.*

To my dismay, I stumbled across another use of the room one day when I came back late and unexpectedly. The regional VP, the lease manager, and the sales manager were in the conference room sitting around a table with a lease and a few implements of dubious purpose sitting in front of them. They were all in the bag, naturally, and having a good old time with their apparent tomfoolery. I overheard the lease manager say that the Wite-Out wouldn't show up on a copy.

"Just don't lay it on too thick," he said as the sales manager bent over the lease trying to focus, the small applicator, caked in white, shaking in his hand.

"We need somebody steadier," the regional VP admonished. "This ain't shake, rattle and roll time," and they all laughed.

When the sales manager came back to his office, I asked him what they were doing in there. "We had ... had to f-f-fix some ... thing up," he told me in his inebriated late-day style, and then he winked at me.

"Fix what?" I innocently inquired.

"A cleric ... a ... cal err ... error," he scoffed, like I'd just shown up on the back of a rutabaga truck.

Later, when I told another salesman about the incident, he smiled and said, "Welcome to the fix-it shop where no lease or contract is safe."

"Why were they changing a lease?" I innocently inquired.

He smiled and walked away, like I was the rutabaga that fell off the truck.

I never found out exactly what they were doing with their covert duplicity in the conference room that night, or any other night, but, over time, their foibles became more and more apparent, like the time I dated the regional VP's ... wait. I'll save that for ... you know. Oh, grow up!

To further my education in corporate hijinks, I moved on to the New York City offices of the largest billboard company in North America. I was in the home office so I had no first-hand knowledge of the kinds of depravity I'd previously encountered, but there was plenty of chicanery still to be enjoyed. Like the time a new VP of national sales was promoted into the corporate headquarters. He had come from one of our largest facilities where he was in charge of the entire operation. I was told he'd practically doubled profitability in that market, which he had a track record of doing as he rapidly advanced his way up the corporate ladder. Because of his stellar reputation, he was eventually recruited away by a competitor, and ended up as the president of a well-known company in an unrelated field. He became semi-well known in certain circles and you may have heard of him.

But not all structures are built on solid foundations, and in this case, doing the right thing was moving up the corporate ladder regardless of the collateral damage.

And there was plenty of collateral damage.

Part of my job was traveling to all our markets and working with the sales groups, and in that capacity I happened to spend some time with the guy who replaced the guy who would someday become semi-well known in certain circles, and he gave me a whole new perspective on moving up the corporate ladder. Evidently, the guy who would someday become semi-well known in certain circles was a master at cutting costs to the bone — upkeep of the billboards and facility, repairs, improvements, raises, paying bills, annoying expenditures like that — and when he left for New York City to eventually become semi-well known in certain circles, he left behind a devastated market and dispirited crew of employees.

He had engendered a *first-class tragic trauma* by letting the market dissipate into a shambled state of decay. This unscrupulous behavior went unnoticed because he was terribly skillful at masking his clever misappropriation of the company's trust, and, to his short-term gain, as a result of his especially talented and manipulative virtuosity at using the company's rapacious need for legerdemain in dexterously dealing with Wall Street. In truth, the company had simply grown too big to manage itself — a condition that has spread throughout so much of our economy, like an insatiable infection eating through the flesh of commerce and into the industrious organs that are supposed to drive our pecuniary enterprises. In other words, the company was like a man who had gotten so fat he couldn't bend over to pick up a $20 bill lying at his feet. The guy who would someday become semi-well known in certain circles understood this principal of inverse-adroitness well and was able to use it to his great advantage, like a tornado blowing through a trailer park.

The trick for the guy who would someday become semi-well known in certain circles was to hit quickly and move on before his deception was discovered, leaving behind the shattered remnants of a market for the next guy to clean up. And the next guy wasn't happy — it took him years to dig out of the hole created by the guy who would someday become semi-well known in certain circles, and the next guy didn't look too good in the company's eyes in spite of his Herculean effort to save the market from complete disaster. It was a no-win situation for the unlucky people who followed the guy who would someday become semi-well known in certain circles.

Unfortunately (or maybe fortunately for the guy gathering material for future scribblings), the guy who would someday become semi-well known in certain circles was not the only person of interest on the upper floors at HQ — oh no, we had a whole corps of them.

As demonstrated the day the CEO showed up unexpectedly one morning. The CEO was supposed to be out of town, but in he walked at his usual 8 a.m., and the place was practically empty. He was accustomed to seeing all the offices and cubicles full of busy, busy worker bees, and he was surprised and disturbed to find the hive moribund on that particular morning.

You see, those worker bees kept a close eye on the CEO's schedule, and when the boss bee (I just didn't want to use "queen bee" because ... well, can you blame me?) was in town, they all buzzed in by 7:45. But when he was away, the bees would sleep late, bumbling in between 9 and 10, after most of the day's best nectar had been sucked dry by their hungry competitors.

It was bee-wildering ...

... to the CEO, and a few heads rolled as a result of that un-bee-lievable bee-devilment.

One head that didn't roll bee-longed (okay, enough) to a guy who came in at close to 11 that morning. I never understood exactly what that guy did except suck up to the CEO. His title was VP of Corporate Communication, whatever that meant, but his real purpose seemed to be to impress people.

Like his crossword puzzles.

He always had The New York Times folded open to the crossword puzzle sitting on the corner of his desk. Unvaryingly, he kept it facing him so you couldn't make out the penciled-in words, but you could see that all the boxes of the puzzle had been completed. For all appearances, he finished the complex and extremely difficult crossword puzzle of The New York Times daily, which made him some kind of genius.

You would think.

But ...

One day when we were meeting in his office about corporate communications (I suppose, even though I didn't know what that meant), he had to leave our meeting for a short time to take care of some emergency corporate communications business. While he was gone, I flipped over the strategically placed newspaper and took a closer look at the crossword puzzle, and you won't believe what I saw: All the words were filled in, for sure, but none of them matched the clues given. Wow! Every day he would have to sit there and figure out words that fit into the number of blocks provided for each clue — without solving any of the clues!

What industry!

What diligence!

What a fraud!

And what a huge waste of time for such a ridiculously deviant affectation. I suppose it called for some kind of genius to hatch a deceptive scheme like that, but that's exactly the kind of bee-zarre bee-havior (sorry) that blurred the lines between doing the right thing and doing the wrong thing in pursuit of the right thing in my Quixotesque quest for success and enlightenment (*and never the twain shall meet?*). One of the most notable things I remember about working in corporate America was that nobody ever talked about right or wrong, only appearances and profitability, or the appearance of profitability.

Or corporate-corporal shenanigans, and that chatter was the currency of choice for the over-libidinous drones with little bee-twixt (slipped out) real and myth.

... talk is cheap when the story is good, and the tales grow taller on down the line.

However, there was nothing mythical about the saga of Sandra and Patrick — I know, I was there. But maybe I'll save that story for *How to Sell the Plague* ... oh, what the hell: We had hired an outside organization to handle fulfillment of our co-op poster program, and Sandra was the point person for the subcontractor. Patrick worked in our print division, where they produced the program. Sandra lived in North Carolina and Patrick had recently arrived from Ireland.

Now this was in the days before Austin Powers schooled America on British slang, so during a meeting one Monday afternoon, Sandra was telling us about her weekend at the beach. Patrick asked Sandra what she liked to do at the beach, and Sandra said she loved to shag.

Patrick fell off his chair.

He was as shocked as Claude Rains because, as we now know, on the British Isles, shag is slang for Fornication Under Consent of the King, or f**k (love those asterisks!). Can you imagine sitting in a meeting with a beautiful young object of your lust who looks you in the eyes and tells you he/she loves to f**k? Asterisks and all!

To poor Patrick's disappointment, Sandra was not talking about sex; she was talking about dancing. At the beach in North Carolina, they listen to a 1950s/1960s style of music referred to locally as beach music, and they do a dance to it something like a slower jitterbug called The Shag (the official dance of North Carolina). So, on a hot Saturday night, while the happy revelers at the beach in North Carolina are shagging their asses off to The Drifters, the good folks in Ireland are shagging their asses off to the thump, thump, thump of old wooden floorboards (the official dance of Ireland).

Here we had Sandra believing she was doing the right thing in sharing her good times, while Patrick was hoping Sandra was going to share some good times with him — the rightest thing Patrick could think of. Meanwhile, Sandra ended up doing the wrong thing inadvertently, and Patrick went home disappointed and frustrated — always the wrong thing.

As you can see, it all gets very confusing, and the difference between right and wrong can be hard to ascertain, like whether I was really going to include this story in *How to Sell the Plague.* Of course not. I was always going to use it here. I was just shagging with you.

All that bee-zarro (last one, I promise) bee-havior (I really mean it this time) I learned in my 20-year career in the corporate world ran counterintuitive to the powerful influences of two Germanic sources that helped form my resilient-yet-nettlesome perspective: my Nana and Helmut and Gerhart. Nana was my mother's mother. Her parents immigrated from Germany mid-19th century and brought with them all the strict efficiency and discipline characteristic in the Teutonic tradition. They passed those immutable traits on to my grandmother, and she to me.

Nana was a full-time housewife back when most women didn't work outside the home. My grandfather immigrated from England in the early part of the 20th century, and together they produced 10 children. One of my uncles used to say that at nighttime, Pop-Pop would say to Nana, "You want to go to sleep, Mary, or what?" And Nana would answer, "What?"

Ha, ha! An old joke, I know, but still funny, and I bet many of you never heard it before.

Anyway, they were a hardy bunch without a lot of money or social standing, but that didn't diminish my grandparents' resolve or pertinacious pride. Pop-Pop would walk two blocks every Sunday morning to the Episcopal church, while Nana would attend service at the Lutheran church a town away. Their principles were not negotiable, and that's what I learned from my grandparents.

Nana was a cleaning machine: She started on Monday morning and, along with the grocery shopping, cooking, laundry and child rearing (and when I say child rearing, the rear is the point of reference from where we learned many of life's important lessons, if you know what I mean), and spent the next five days going from room to room, floor to floor, sweeping and dusting and scrubbing and disinfecting and keeping that house in perfect order. Then the next Monday, she would start all over again. She was very serious about the entire enterprise, and God forbid if you left a coffee cup ring on the kitchen table.

It was contagious. I had an aunt who was so neurotic about cleaning that if you smoked a cigarette in her house, every time you put an ash in the ashtray, she'd jump up and clean it. If you smoked an entire cigarette in front of her, she'd get a real workout jumping up and running to the kitchen trash can and back. What a hoot!

So, cleanliness was an important staple of my youth, along with other interesting dictums handed down from on high. Nana, in her uncompromising elegance, pounded into my limited consciousness to always do the right thing, like stay away from those Irish and Italian kids.

"Those Catholic boys will do nothing but get you in trouble," she'd lecture me. So guess who I ended up hanging out with in my teenage years of discovery and rebellion? Did you guess the no-good kids from Sacred Heart? Correctomundo! And you know what? Nana was right — my fellow Italian (long "I") and Irish mobsters and I got into plenty of healthy trouble together, and although I didn't always (maybe "seldom" might be more apt) do the right thing, I certainly learned the difference during my colorful youth.

I wouldn't trade those experiences for money, and I often wonder if Nana didn't purposely push me toward those boys and all the gritty reality of life in contrast to the Norman Rockwell-seeming gentility of my hometown.

In my little town, I grew up believing, God keeps his eye on us all.

And in my little town, Nana was God.

If I got my bachelor's degree in doing the right thing from Nana, I got my master's from Helmut and Gerhart, owners of the Wienerstube Restaurant in Aspen, Colorado, where I spent part of my wasted youth working. Helmut and Gerhart were German-trained, Austrian chefs who were as proficient and competent as anybody I ever worked with. And they were a merciless combo, playing good cop/bad cop. Helmut (because I believe it came naturally to him following in the footsteps of another Austrian who moved to Germany) was the bad cop, and he could freeze you with a look of scornful disgust. He was good at looking repulsed, but not so good when he tried to smile. Actually, his smile could freeze you, too, being an eerie, gap-toothed, crooked precursor to Jack Nicholson's Joker, who I met at the Wienerstube, along with a plethora of other notables and a few not-as-notable-as-they-once-were.

Gerhart, on the other side of the looking glass, was a pleasure to work for. He was a nice man with an ingratiating personality who tried to smooth out all the wrinkles Helmut left in his wake. On more than one occasion after Helmut threatened to fire me for some indiscretion like accidently splashing a scintilla of soap into the rinsing sink, Gerhart would pat me on the back and tell me not to worry about it, that I was doing a fine job. He always said, "fine job," never "good job." Do you find that curious ... like he never wanted to contradict Helmut, like they were a precision tag team, like we were being played?

If so, then being played was okay with me because I loved that job. I was a dishwasher who also handled some food prep, making a buck-and-a-half an hour, with time-and-a-half for overtime, and there was plenty of overtime if I wanted it, which I did when I wasn't suffering from the residual damage of the poisonous agave plant. Every day at 4 p.m., Helmut and Gerhart would close the restaurant for an hour and serve a family-style, sit-down meal for all the employees. Even on my days off I could come in for supper. Plus, all the beer I could drink (even when I was working — they were German trained, after all), all the food I wanted whenever I wanted, not to mention about 30 young, sweet waitresses looking for an adventure.

Just call me the adventurer.

I learned so much that summer when I wasn't out adventuring. The Wienerstube used all copper-bottom pots and pans, but cleaning those suckers with soap and water wouldn't do. Oh no, we used salt and vinegar to scrub those babies until they *were glowing like a metal on the edge of a knife.* You might lose a layer or two of epidermis, but those pots and pans were the pride of the place, and Helmut checked them out closely at the end of the day like he was inspecting a squad of the Waffen-SS.

Those guys were meticulous. They once hired a cook to help out during the busy summer season, but he didn't last long. He had been trained in New York City, which in itself was enough to make Helmut scrunch up his brow and wrinkle his nose in sanctimonious repugnance. Unfortunately for the New Yorker, he had learned to crack an egg with one hand, but at the Wienerstube, you used two hands. No questions asked and no wiggle room when it came to chancing even a sliver of eggshell in the dish. So bye-bye ... what was your name again? That noise you hear walking out the door is the sound of one hand clapping.

The best job at the Wienerstube — nay, the best job I ever had in my life — was working in the bakery with Helmut first thing in the morning. They had the ingredients for the dessert menu shipped in from all over the world, and if you were assigned the morning shift, you got to help Helmut construct all those glorious gastronomical delights, such as Black Forest gateau or apple strudel smothered in powdered sugar. Yum, yum! The smell alone was overwhelmingly magnificent, and just the thought of walking into the bakery at dawn still puts a smile on my face and a glow in my ... stomach.

Helmut and Gerhart always did the right thing when it came to running their restaurant, and once I got past their Gestapo-like HR practices, I had the time of my life at their hands, learning so much, eating so much, drinking so much, adventuring so much ...

I probably never thanked them, and I probably never thanked my Nana, but I owe a great deal of gratitude for their contribution to the person I would become and the successes I would enjoy. There's this meme going around that I believe sums up what I learned from them: "Integrity is doing the right thing even when nobody is looking."

But what's the right thing?

When it all boils down to the brown spot at the bottom of the pot (that would have driven Helmut crazy and given me great joy), that's an easy one. Another guy who became semi-well known in certain circles wrote this many years ago, and there's no simpler, no truer answer: "This above all: to thine own self be true, and it must follow, as the night the day, thou canst not then be false to any man."

What can I add to that? Only that I hope you enjoy the book ... no, not that one; the one you're holding in your hands.

Try to keep up.

3

Sales Ethics — Not an Oxymoron (Really!)

I have occasion to visit a certain beach town in South Jersey that has a reputation for being a bit elitist. What it really is, however, is an island full of silly men.

And frivolous women.

A true testament to the fortunes of accidental birth. Tanned, prep-school postured, Grey Goose VX swilling, Beemer-encrusted, puerile-smiling, empty IZOD-garbed twits romping through the glory of daddy's and mumsy's largesse, or the recipients of much-manufactured luck in the oft-rigged gambling industry known as Wall Street.

A whole island of them.

Okay, that's an exaggeration, but not by much. At least not regarding the property owners, the NEW property owners of the too-much-is-never-enough orthodoxy, building monuments to their collective need for voracious vacuous validation, playing in shifting sand on eroding dunes of misguided aspirations.

Very sad.

Because as they chase the demons of not-keeping-up-with-the-Joneses, they are wiping out an entire seaside tradition, our tradition, the heritage of summertime pilgrimages by the hoi polloi as *they that go down to the sea in* ... minivans.

We would pack up the old family transporter, *à la* Clark Griswold, and head to a rented seashore cottage to spend a week or two living on seafood, cheesesteaks, frozen custard and fudge — especially fudge; playing miniature golf and pinochle; romping on the beach all day until the last speck of light melted into the ocean's choppy horizon, getting painfully sunburned in preparation for latter-day skin cancers, being rough and tumbled by the thunderous waves, dragged out to sea by an unforgiving undertow, stung by unseen jellyfish, incessantly accosted by lifeguards and attacked by seagulls in hot pursuit of our PB&Js.

Good times.

But that's all changing as the Main Liners descend like seven-year locust, only these pests never leave. They eat their way through the old cottages, leveling them to the not-so-terra-firma, and in the shadow of thousands of cherished memories, erect hollow monstrosities, soulless castles with the *feng shui* of mausoleums.

So on a recent trip, when the garish opulence was getting the better of me, I jumped on my trusty bicycle for a two-wheeled expedition of sublimation. I navigated the rickety old causeways of our grandparents and the new concrete spans of delusion and ventured out onto the mainland where they drive pickup trucks and eat Hamburger Helper.

Welcome home.

As I peddled into Middle America, I serendipitously came across a paved trail, a trail that beckoned me to new adventures of losing my way, something I excel at on my modern-day velocipede. Accordingly, after riding for only a few miles and exploring interesting-looking offshoots and pathways, I ended up at that old familiar place: thoroughly lost. I hadn't a clue where I was when I found myself in the middle of a large sports complex. But not just any sports complex; this was the most remarkable, spacious collection of fields of dreams I had ever come across.

I was blown away by its simple magnificence.

The landscape was full of manicured baseball diamonds of various sizes to accommodate all levels of the grand old game, all with outfield fences complete with local advertisements, aluminum bleachers, covered dugouts, electric scoreboards, snack bars and paved parking lots. The playing surfaces were beautiful: green, green grass that must have been watered daily and perfectly cut-out base paths, raked and pristine. As I pedaled my way around the facility in utter amazement, I couldn't find one single piece of litter — not even an old cigarette butt.

Wow! I couldn't help but marvel at the time and energy it must have taken the parents, volunteers and municipal workers who put this place together and who maintained it in such a noble manner. All for the enjoyment of kids. What a marvelous testament to hard work and altruistic industry, juxtaposed to my fellow island occupants, who couldn't build their palaces big enough to ever scratch that itch. Meanwhile, the assiduous mainlanders slept soundly only a few miles yonder, but light years away in expressions of self-worth.

And it occurred to me as I made my way back to the land of broken toys, this is what sales is all about: You can make the choice to go for the money and end up with nothing of real value, or you can make the choice to help people and create value.

And sleep well.

The ethics of selling boil down to three simple rules:

1. Treat others the way you want to be treated.
2. Always be honest and sell with integrity.
3. Help people.

Long before we had social media to teach us how to behave, Hillel the Elder explained the Torah to a Gentile thusly: "What is hateful to you, do not do to your fellow. This is the whole Torah; the rest is explanation." That is, of course, the veritable Golden Rule, and life really is that simple: Be kind to others. Period.

Regarding Rule 2, Benjamin Franklin famously said, "Honesty is the best policy." He said that about 250 years ago, and you know what? It's still true, maybe even more so today. My main man Zig Ziglar added, "The most important persuasion tool you have in your entire arsenal is integrity."

And when it comes to helping others, the Zigmeister said,

"You can have everything in life you want, if you will just help other people get what they want."

Three rules that are both simple and as complicated as the universe itself.

But all attainable if you make the right choices.

As for me, we will load up the old front-wheel drive sleigh to once again embrace the frothy majesty of the sea and revel in the good company of fellowship. And we will ignore the scions of synthetic affluence with their edifices of narcissism and continue to bask in the simple pleasures of sunburn, jellyfish and hostile seagulls.

Because that's the choice we make.

4

Liar, Liar, Pants on Fire

Fake news is in the news, but that's probably fake news.

In its July 2-9, 2018 issue, Sports Illustrated featured Lonnie Walker IV in its Point After section. He was the 18th pick in the 2018 NBA draft, coming out of the University of Miami where he played for only one year but helped the Hurricanes reach the NCAA tournament. The year before, Walker was playing at Reading High School, leading the team to a Pennsylvania state championship. My wife graduated from Reading High and was a huge basketball fan back in the Stu Jackson era, so we followed Mssr. Walker et al. with great interest. The young man's a terrific basketball talent, and on top of that, Sports Illustrated dubbed him the most interesting rookie in the world — not the most fascinatingly creative or the most resolutely obtuse or the most consummate connoisseur of fake news, but the most interesting rookie in the world.

And that's very interesting.

Because one of the questions SI asked him was whether he believes (in) the moon landings. He answered, "The background, the surroundings — y'all tried to make it look too much like a moon. The details were almost too great. There's no way it looks this nice or this well done."

So, if I understand Professor Walker correctly, the moon landings were fake because the moon didn't look fake enough?

Now that's interesting.

But maybe not such a stretch for young sky-Walker when you consider he's about to enter the fakest of all fake worlds: professional sports, a world where the beauty of the game and the nobility of honest competition have lost their appeal to a great sector of its fan base, a base that is much more focused on odds and point spreads and over/unders. And even more insidious, fantasy sports, the quite-possibly last step in mankind's rather rapid decay back to the level of awareness and enlightenment of the one-cell organisms from which it came.

As Carl Sagan once put it, billions and billions of folding-stuff is fried-out on spurious equivalents that are antithetical to the purity of the proposed intent and function of the enterprise. In other words, the actual outcome of sporting events has become subordinate, if not irrelevant, to the wants and needs of the degenerate multitudes' misdirected passion for fake events.

And it gets worse, as we learn from the *ad infinitum* reruns of *Seinfeld*. It seems there's been more faking going on in the private arenas of copulated commerce than on any playing field or court. In an episode titled "The Mango," when Elaine informs Jerry, in all her inimitable warmth, that she faked it with him, he pleads, incredulously, "What about the breathing, the panting, the moaning, the screaming?"

"Fake, fake, fake, fake," Elaine responds, emphasizing each "fake" with a stroke of her index finger, like counting off strawberries on your shortcake.

Is nothing sacred?

Apparently not. But, hey, if you listen to the hysteria coming out of the platitudinous orifices of the overstimulated and underinformed denizens of the brave new world and their designated town criers (and aren't they admirably living up to that moniker lately), we're in the throes of a dishonesty epidemic perpetrated by fake-newsers gone wild, the likes of which we've never seen before.

I think not.

If twerking is art, reality TV shows such as *Naked and Afraid* are entertainment and Kevin Costner is an actor, can a little fake news really be considered a new phenomenon? (I know, I know, you Kevin Costner-lovers have your knickers in a knot over that one, the dissing of the great expressionless monotone theslesspian. I'm not saying he was never good in anything. On the contrary, he was great in *The Big Chill*. Don't remember him in it? He played Alex Marshall, the dead guy, and he was marvelous — he was born to play dead.)

No folks, fake news has always been with us. Thomas Jefferson, in effect, bought an editorial platform to make up slanderous stuff about John Adams during the election of 1800; Abraham Lincoln issued the Emancipation Proclamation under the guise of humanity, but its true purpose was to prevent foreign powers from assisting the Confederacy; Lee Harvey Oswald shot John F. Kennedy.

'Nuff said?

Fake news has been our birthright since the inception of this star-spangled experiment and should have been included in the Declaration of Independence along with life, liberty and the pursuit of happiness. Alas, we used to be less manipulatively excitable in those bygone days before social media did our thinking for us, before we became so adamantly shrill. And that shrill has become the current definition of fake news: Whatever you believe that is not in agreement with what I believe is fake news, and the louder I shout it, the faker it is.

So there!

Not since Dr. Samuel Johnson kicked the stone and said, "I refute it thus," has there been so much debate over what is real and what is fake. But let's face it, it's hard to keep it real in an incessantly shifting environment of smoke and mirrors, especially if you're trying to win friends and influence people ... something I learned years ago when I was a young pup sales puke trying to get noticed, and the notice I coveted most was a gold Rolex watch and a Mercedes Benz 280 SL — a hot little two-seater in maroon with natural-leather tan seats.

It was down the shore one summer during that embryonic period of my life when I chanced to meet a fellow in possession of a gold Rolex watch and a Mercedes Benz 280 SL — a hot little two-seater in maroon with natural-leather tan seats. We were introduced by a young woman of superior bone structure and other superior structures I fancied in a hot, humid, crowded bar with tepid beer and mean mosquitoes. In the midst of that infested inferno, the guy was slick and silky, so cool he could smooth the "o" out of Cheeris, and I greatly admired his style and accoutrements.

Once we got to know each other, he confided in me that the Rolex was a knockoff, a fake he had purchased from a street vendor in New York City, and the Benz was leased — a relatively new concept back then — at a low monthly installment with a huge, daunting balloon payment due at the end of the lease. As it turned out, the monthly nut for his expensive ride was about the same as mine for my economical and low-profile Subaru, sans the balloon payment and associated angst.

Fake, fake, fake, fake!

So when it comes to fake, I take the advice of the great American theoretician, Groucho Marx: "The secret of life is honesty and fair dealing. If you can fake that, you've got it made."

5

Marching Onward

T.S. Eliot was wrong.

April is not the cruelest month. In Eliot's signature poem, "The Waste Land," an opaque trip of obscure images and arcane quotes (in a variety of languages, just in case you missed one of Eliot's major themes: that he's smarter than you), he draws a metaphorical juxtaposition of the deconstruction of man while nature renews itself every spring, obsessing over depression, anxiety, alienation, impotence and all that other really cool stuff he enjoyed.

But he was wrong. April is not the cruelest month — March is.

Every year, we inhabitants of the northern tier of this transitionally dynamic space rock that's rapidly deteriorating into a miasma of hyperbole and hysteria, excitedly anticipate March cometh like the great emancipator of all that's mundane and unwholesome: movies too weak for major release dates, inane TV shows aimed at the galactically witless (guess who?), self-congratulatory awards programs preached at us by the dark doyens of depravity, not to mention a mess of vitamin D deficiency.

As the old saw goes, March comes in like a lion and goes out like a lamb (or as John Belushi put it on *Saturday Night Live* — when it was still funny, before it decomposed into silly, doltish callousness — March comes in like an emu and goes out like a tapir). Despite this dog-eared bromide of banal wisdom, we greet March each year with great expectations of renewed life, lifted spirits and as a milestone of hope and promise — hope and promise right now, not in three or four weeks after it morphs into a tapir.

Self-appointed wise people who always know the wrong thing to say will tell you that spring doesn't officially begin until the vernal equinox on either the 20th or 21st of the month, regardless of what some furry rodent predicts, and from a meteorological point of view, March is a winter month.

Hogwash.

The National Weather Service categorizes winter as the time between the beginning of December through the end of February and lists March as a spring month.

So there, all you buzzkill balloon poppers.

We all want March to be the slayer of winter, a time to put away the snow shovels and get out the sunscreen, to don-we-now our unencumbering, gaily decorated summer apparel and roll down the car windows and blast the radio (an electronic audio device, for you millennials). But alas, good times seldom spring forth in the cruelest month as we trudge through the last vestige of cold and windy despair, searching hopefully for that first robin redbreast or crocus bud popping its head out from the frozen tundra of our *winterzeit die Schwermut* (with a wink to Old Possum, that in case you didn't know was T.S. Eliot's nickname, who in case you didn't know wrote *Book of Practical Cats,* which in case you didn't know was the basis for the show *Cats,* that in case you didn't know was a smash Broadway hit musical that ran for years, and in case you didn't know was never made into a video game so you probably never heard of it.)

Which is, by the way (and my point, finally), the best part of the human spirit: our steadfast resolve as a people to keep marching onward when all seems bleak and hopeless and arduously endless.

March defines who we are.

And nowhere is that definition more apt than in the wonderful world of sales, where *we few, we happy few,* remain defiantly energetic in the face of daily disappointment and setbacks, indifferent and rude customers, compassion-challenged bosses, impossible quotas and deadlines, ineffective products and moth-eaten territories, and yet, misunderstood and reviled, we assiduously march forth into the cave of the dragon every day with a smile on our face and a song in our heart.

And all that jazz.

I was recently reminded of this by a young woman in one of my training classes who was new to sales and struggling, tormented by her fear of failure and full of self-doubt, unable, or more accurately, unwilling to step out of herself and use one of the best tools available to salespeople: empathy. She was stuck in her own agenda and couldn't see over the walls of those self-imposed limitations. Her perspective was all about her and the obsessive and omnipotent dread of rejection.

We had been talking after classes about her problems, and I was working with her to better organize her objectives and strengthen her focus. After several weeks, she came in one day and greeted me with a big smile and a twinkle in her eye.

"What's up?" I asked. "You look positively positive."

"Things are going much better! I'm finally making some sales and starting to hit my numbers," she gushed.

She went on to tell me what had changed her attitude and helped her turn the corner. She had pitched a prospect and he had signed the contract and given her a check: her first sale! She was beside herself with delight, and her manager made a big deal out of the occasion, publicly congratulating her in front of the entire sales team.

Sadly, the check bounced and she was forced to go back and confront the prospect. When she asked him why he had given her a bad check, he told her he was so impressed with her energy and commitment that he got carried away and felt compelled to buy her product. He told her she was a great saleswoman and that she had totally convinced him she could help his business. He thought he could cover the check, but things were slow, and he just got caught up in her enthusiasm.

"And that didn't crush you?" I asked.

"Just the opposite," she responded. "It hit me like a brick to the face that if I could sell a guy with no money, think what I could do with somebody with money. It was a real epiphany."

In other words, when things were at their worst, she was at her best. Facing failure head-on can do that for you.

Just like we face March, armed with optimism but ready to fight the good fight into another reawakening of hope eternal — March's promise. That is, as long as you don't buy into another Belushi-ism that says March comes in like a worm-eating fernbird and goes out like a worm-eating fernbird. In fact, the whole year is like a worm-eating fernbird.

Talk about March madness.

6

Relax, Nothing is Under Control

Control is an illusion.

Or as Dr. Claire Lewicki (played by Nicole Kidman) in *Days of Thunder* put it when talking to race car driver Cole Trickle (played by Tom Cruise), "Control is an illusion, you infantile egomaniac. Nobody knows what's gonna happen next: not on a freeway, not in an airplane, not inside our own bodies and certainly not on a racetrack with 40 other infantile egomaniacs."

Okay, so we're not all race car drivers fighting for the ultimate control over life and death, but most of us spend a great deal of our lives chasing that same illusion of having control where none is available.

Take my wife ...

Please.

Out in public, people believe I'm king of the castle. They think I rule the roost, that I wear the pants in the family.

Ha!

It's an illusion. Back at the ranch, I am controlless. Oh, she lets me believe I have control, such as with the TV remote. But do we ever watch women's beach volleyball, or *Family Guy*, or Amy Schumer?

No.

Do we ever order anchovy pizza with jalapeno peppers?

No.

Do we ever go to tractor pulls or naked mud wrestling?

No.

Do we ever sit around in our underwear all day Sunday

drinking beer and watching football?

Well, yes, but that's a religious experience, and I'm still allowed freedom of religion under the Constitution (as long as it's okay with her).

Think I'm kidding? A while back, I bought a new Jeep Cherokee without consulting Her Nibs. I loved that maroon-with-black-accents four by four, tooling around the mountains looking for mud or deep snow.

She hated it.

Not so much the vehicle as the color. She hated the maroon with black accents.

How do I know?

Because she told me every day for the duration of my rather short but painful relationship with the macho-muscle descendant of the Willy's-Overland Motor Company. I wanted that utility vehicle in the worst way. She didn't. Guess who won?

Ah yes, *a constant battle for the ultimate state of control,* a battle you can never win.

So why do so many sales training programs emphasize the need for gaining control over prospects during a sales meeting? Why do they spend so much time hammering salespeople with the idea that controlling the interviewing process is the key to the kingdom?

Why do they sell on TV cooking pans that never stick, until you actually use them, that is?

Because some people will believe anything as long as it comes packaged in bright colorful paper with pretty ribbons and bows. And big sales training companies specialize in attractive and appealing wrappings that disguise their true intent: to get you to give them your money. They do that by promising to teach you how they do what they do so you can get other people to do what you do. It's a nifty game of illusion — watch the hypnotic bouncing ball as I deftly pick your pocket while promising to teach you how to pick pockets. Like the old scam of placing an ad saying, "Send me $2 and I'll mail you the secret of how to get people to send you $2."

Forget control. It doesn't exist. As Zoë B puts it in simplelifestrategies.com, "... there is actually no such thing as control. We are never in control. Ever. The happiest and most successful people dance to the rhythm of life and they look at each challenge or each thing that is out of their control as an opportunity to shine. They adapt and they mold into the circumstances that are thrown at them! They sure as hell don't try and control them! How ludicrous to try and control something that cannot be controlled! What an utter waste of time! And the irony is that the more they let go and go with the flow, the more control they actually have over their lives."

In other words, you can only gain control when you stop trying to gain control.

What a concept!

Like when I was a young man riding horses. As I came to learn, horses can be extremely stubborn animals, and once in a while you can have great difficulty getting them to go where you want them to go. There's an expression in horseback riding that goes, "Give the horse its head," which means when a horse is fighting you for control, let go of the reins and let him move in the direction he wants to take you. After a few steps, he begins to think he has control and at that point, becomes more pliable; then you can take back the reins and be on your way.

Happy trails to you.

Also, if you're ever lost and are desperately trying to regain control of your trip, give the horse his head and he will invariably take you home.

No muss, no fuss.

So the moral of this story is that true control comes only when you stop fighting for control. Sailors don't fight the wind; they don't try to bend the wind to their will. Instead, they adjust the sails and use what the wind gives them to achieve their objective.

Control is an illusion. Forget it. Trust and respect are what you should be aiming for because those are the true keys to the kingdom. If you want to win friends and influence people, give them their head, and they'll bring you back to the barn every time.

7

The Brand-New Same Old

When I was young, I liked to watch cowboy movies. In many of those movies — the ones about real cowboys — there'd invariably be a scene where the cowpoke would round up the calves and, with a metal branding iron heated to a red-hot glow, burn their ranch's brand into the baby bovines' hides.

Ouch!

When I was in college, we had a chapter of Omega Psi Phi fraternity on campus. Once a year, Omega would round up its pledges, and, with a metal branding iron heated to a red-hot glow, burn the Greek letter for Omega into the young neophytes' arms.

Double ouch!

And that was the extent of my knowledge about branding until I left the ivy-covered halls of enlightenment and ventured forth into the world of making a living. The mode of making a living that chose me was selling advertising, so for the next 35 years, I reported daily to the mill of make-believe to toil at the perfidious task of selling toilet paper and frozen chicken patties.

That's where I learned about top-of-mind awareness, a phrase we were stuck with until some supercilious, job-justifying marketing wizard brewed up a batch of misdirection and invented the cool-sounding yet duplicitous distinction dubbed "branding," a new word for an old idea that has been around since the ancient Egyptians were building the first roadside billboards known as obelisks.

In theory, branding is a nebulous term used to justify all

likes of marketing initiatives that present no unique selling propositions or content relative to distinguishing features and benefits. It's simply getting your name out there and a terrific vehicle for creative directors to soar untethered in pursuit of awards and industry recognition.

In application, branding is one of the most misunderstood concepts in business, which is a mystery because it's not that complicated. It's marketing sans a specific pitch or call to action, a reinforcement of your name or brand, designed to solicit an emotional response, generally one of familiarity and comfort, a rather vague positioning statement from 30,000 feet without being saddled with the burdensome responsibility of actually selling product.

In other words, advertising lite.

Mystery solved.

Easy peasy.

But yet, so difficult for so many companies.

For every home run, the base paths of product identity are littered with the copious corpses of poorly conceived, poorly developed, poorly executed or poorly placed branding campaigns: for every Kleenex, Xerox and Google — products that were branded so strongly that they became synonymous with their product's category — there are the DeLorean, Sony Betamax and the electric fork. But the biggest flop in history came at the hands of one of the best branding companies in the world: Coca-Cola.

Back in the 1980s, as the world was busy discovering computer imaging and distracted by all its exciting possibilities, product research and development was replaced as the engine that drove profitability by the myopic and craven notion that marketing could and should dictate corporate strategy — decide how much money you want to make and then position your product to achieve that bean-counter, narrowly restrictive approach to progress.

Enter New Coke.

The Coca-Cola Company was losing market share to Pepsi,

considered by most folks to be a sweeter-tasting cola. So rather than attempt to strengthen its brand through a targeted marketing program, Coca-Cola decided to jeopardize its No. 1 position in the marketplace and copy the competition.

As a result, on April 23, 1985, it introduced a reformulated, sweeter soft drink that immediately created a firestorm of protest and consumer backlash. Quicker than you could say "the real thing," old Coke was brought back and rebranded as Coca-Cola Classic, and in relatively short order, New Coke disappeared from grocery store shelves and the American lexicon.

Forever.

Today, the original sugary, caffeinated promoter of tooth decay, obesity, liver disease, Type 2 diabetes, cancer and many other wondrous mutations continues to teach the world to sing.

Oh sure, it may be a dirge, but we're singing in harmony, nonetheless.

Chug, chug, chug.

Unlike New Coke, a couple of brands come to mind that created identities that sustain images ingrained in our culture. The Marlboro Man was a staple of the second half of the 20th century, a cowboy carrying a saddle or other western paraphernalia, and smoking a Marlboro. The image was so strong that by the 1970s, Marlboro had pretty much eschewed all copy other than the picture of a cowboy and the word "Marlboro." The campaign worked because it delivered a consistent message in support of a product that held real value for consumers — that is, if you're willing to overlook a few pesky foibles such as lung cancer, emphysema, heart disease and other annoying afflictions that ended up killing many of the Marlboro cowboy models.

Nike also was able to capitalize on a strong image cultivated with pictures of popular athletes in action. Like Marlboro, Nike used very little copy and instead relied heavily on recognizable archetypes to promote its identity of superior, performance-enhancing sportswear. And like Marlboro, Nike delivered a consistent message that promoted quality products, products brought to you by the good folks offering prepubescents exciting employment opportunities in sweatshops all around the Third World.

So take lessons from these large, international conglomerates if you want to establish your product or service: When it comes to branding, the most important considerations are product viability and consistency of message, two considerations missed by BIC when it inexplicably tried to introduce disposable women's underwear. The product didn't work because it was such a dramatic departure from the image BIC had spent years cultivating: a producer of inexpensive and disposable pens, lighters and razors. In the end, the product placement confused consumers, and it didn't satisfy any needs or solve any problems. Also, the entire concept was a bit creepy.

Unfortunately for BIC, disposable underwear was an idea whose time had yet to come, and no manner of aggressive branding can cover up that kind of utilitarian deficiency. If only it had realized that the same baby boomers who had supported its mercurial growth would soon need a disposable undergarment, it may have been able to flick that BIC into the black.

8

Vote for Me, I'll Set You Free

*R*ead my lips: no new taxes.

Oops!

Politicians say the darndest things.

Like the primal scream of presidential hopeful Howard Dean in 2004 that abruptly ended his campaign.

"Yeeaarrgghh!"

Which is what I suppose John Kerry should have said instead of, "I actually did vote for the $87 billion, before I voted against it."

Then there was Mitt Romney, who I'm sure wishes he was preoccupied helping Al Gore invent the internet as he freefell when talking about the 47 percent of people he assumed would vote for President Obama no matter what: "These are people who pay no income tax ... my job is not to worry about those people. I'll never convince them they should take personal responsibility and care for their lives."

Yeeaarrgghh, indeed.

In the current manifestations of Michael Dukakis and Sarah Palin, the gaffes are coming at us fast and furious. With so many candidates on the Republican side trying to claw their way out of the morass, and a few usurpers on the Democrat side jockeying for a Cabinet position or ambassadorship, the rhetoric is robust and flamboyant.

And speaking of robust and flamboyant, along come Donald Trump and Bernie Sanders.

Yea!

Then we have Ben Carson's tongue-twisted alienation of a

quarter of the world's population in one fell sound bite.

Or Hillary Clinton chiming in with doublespeak gems like, "I never took a position on Keystone until I took a position on Keystone."

Pretty good, but *if there is four guys, and you're Ringo ...*

So I was pretty excited when Bobby Gunther Walsh of NewsRadio790 WAEB in Pennsylvania's Lehigh Valley asked me to evaluate the candidates from a sales perspective.

For a sales guy who's spent many years studying the art of influence and persuasion, watching politicians during an election cycle is equivalent to Pavlov working in a dog kennel — I was salivating all over myself at the anticipated treat.

Like a fly to honey.

Like a moth to flame.

Like a bull to china shop.

That's because politicians are salespeople with the same objectives as salespeople — to sell themselves. They both use the same principles: Make a good first impression, gain trust, learn who their audience is, discover what the voter wants and needs, deliver a message with conviction and sincerity, and close the deal. Truth be told, some politicians would be much more effective and win elections if they were better disciplined in those time-honored fundamentals, maybe even reading a book or two and taking a course on the art of selling.

One of those basic fundamentals that Donald Trump and Bernie Sanders have used so effectively is a concept called pattern interrupt. A pattern interrupt is exactly what it sounds like: a statement or position that interrupts an expected pattern of behavior. In any given selling situation, the two parties involved (the buyer and the seller) adopt archetypical personas: the aggressive seller and the defensive buyer.

In The Sales Pro Blog, Johnny Bravo writes, "The ultimate goal of a pattern interrupt is to get the person you're speaking with thinking about something other than you being a salesperson." In other words, the objective of a pattern interrupt is to jolt a buyer out of his comfortable position, forcing him to listen and hear what you are saying rather than putting it on autopilot, like a bobblehead doll, smiling and nodding along to your tread-worn recitation of rhetorical pomposity.

"The technique is to do or say something unexpected which disrupts their normal pattern. These types of pattern-breaking techniques originally stem from something called neuro-linguistic programming (NLP)," Bravo adds.

According to Robert B. Dilts at NLP University, "NLP is a multi-dimensional process that involves the development of behavioral competence and flexibility, but also involves strategic thinking and an understanding of the mental and cognitive processes behind behavior. NLP provides tools and skills for the development of states of individual excellence, but it also establishes a system of empowering beliefs and presuppositions about what human beings are, what communication is and what the process of change is all about."

Huh?

Okay, it's based on the science of human behavior — I get it. But in its simplest application, the tool is only effective in the hands of those who know how to use it to their advantage, and that's where politicians like Trump and Sanders fall short.

A pattern interrupt should get the attention of the people you're speaking to so that you can then proceed to sell them on your ideas. In sales, an outrageous statement such as "I'm sure you have no time to talk to me today" is unexpected and different from what the buyer is used to hearing. You say it to get the prospect's attention, but once you do, you use that newfound attention to present yourself in a logical and reasonable manner in order to gain trust and close the sale. What you don't do is keep hammering away with one outrageous statement after another. If you do, you lose credibility fast and slip into the land of flake.

So instead of "Now that I have your attention, folks, let me tell you what I would do," we hear the echo of Ronald Reagan's admonishment to Jimmy Carter, "There you go again!"

Donald and Bernie may live in Flakeland, but at least they make an effort, as opposed to the white noise coming out of the mouths of most of the other presidential hopefuls. Those arrogant angling aspirants appear to live by the credo of the king of pattern interrupt, comedian Steven Wright: "Eagles may soar, but weasels don't get sucked into jet engines."

9

Everywhere There's Lots of Piggies

How do you start a small business?

Start a large business with the help of a bank and wait six months.

Okay, an old joke for sure, and a wee bit cynical, but still resonates because it has a ring of truth to it.

I know from personal experience, very painful personal experience. I had two business loans with large, reputable banks put into workout for no apparent reason other than the banks didn't want to be in the small-business loan sector any longer. Both loans were contracted with local "friendly banks" (an oxymoron if there ever was one) that were gobbled up by larger, even friendlier banks that didn't care that we had never missed a payment (had never even been late), were solvent and making money, and were an honorable, loyal customer.

No sir, didn't matter a lick. They had become undesirous of our business because it wasn't profitable enough, and so they found technicalities to put us into workout. For those of you unfamiliar with the term "workout," it means: "Dear Customer: Please find a way to pay off your loan now or we will destroy your business, ruin your credit, take your collateral (what's left of it), and sell your children into involuntary servitude. Thank you for banking with us."

With the doublespeakesque invocation of "too big to fail" in 2008, banks became the villains of Wall Street, exposing the industry's stalwarts of insatiability as diabolical, avaricious money-grubbers, interested only in increasing their own wealth with none of the ordinary inhibitions of a social consciousness usually associated with being a human being.

And how did that TARP thing work out for us non-piggies?

As Matt Taibbi wrote in Rolling Stone on January 4, 2013: "So what exactly did the bailout accomplish? It built a banking system that discriminates against community banks, makes Too Big to Fail banks even Too Bigger to Failier [sic], increases risk, discourages sound business lending and punishes savings by making it even easier and more profitable to chase high-yield investments than to compete for small depositors. The bailout has also made lying on behalf of our biggest and most corrupt banks the official policy of the United States government. And if any one of those banks fails, it will cause another financial crisis, meaning we're essentially wedded to that policy for the rest of eternity — or at least until the markets call our bluff, which could happen any minute now. Other than that, the bailout was a smashing success."

Thomas Jefferson, in his legendary opposition to Alexander Hamilton's vision of a controlling bank system, saw it coming when he said, "I believe that banking institutions are more dangerous to our liberties than standing armies."

And it wasn't just the big piggies such as Goldman Sachs and Citigroup *crawling in the dirt ... in their starched white shirts.* I was banking with a regional bank that received $300 million in TARP money, money that we were told was to be used for lending purposes, specifically targeted to small business. I tried to get $25,000 of that money but was denied. Instead, the bank used *our* money to buy another bank, enriching the principals involved and making them very piggie-happy.

Banks can be mysterious and difficult institutions to understand or deal with, so here are a few tips that may help:

Banks are in the business of making money, and they make money by moving money from one place to another. Peter puts his money in the bank for safekeeping and the bank pays him some money for the privilege of keeping his money in its bank for safekeeping. In turn, the bank loans Peter's money to Paul, and charges Paul much more than it pays Peter for allowing Paul to use Peter's money.

Banks also make money by investing the float. Float is the time span from when you make a deposit until the bank releases those funds into your account. It can take from one to five business days for those funds to be made available to you, and, in the meantime, the bank puts that money into short-term investments. That's called playing the float. (Sounds like a game at a casino, doesn't it? Now you're catching on.)

When you play the float — writing a check you won't have to cover for a couple of days until it hits your bank — it's called check kiting, and banks don't like that. As a matter of fact, it's illegal and they can put you in jail for it. Woody Guthrie sang about Pretty Boy Floyd, the Robin Hood-like outlaw of the 1930s who had a penchant for robbing banks, "Some will rob you with a six-gun and some with a fountain pen." The difference being that they shoot you or put you in jail if you use a gun, but you a get a big house in the Hamptons if your weapon of choice is a pen.

Doesn't seem fair, does it?

Like bookies, banks get a vigorish every time your money comes or goes, and also, like a bookie, they don't really care if you make money or lose money, as long as they make money. That's because they are not investors: They are bankers with no skin in the game other than the bother it will take to foreclose on your property.

Something else to keep in mind: Banks only loan money to people who can prove they don't need it. As Mark Twain put it, "A banker is a fellow who lends you his umbrella when the sun is shining, but wants it back the minute it begins to rain."

So if you're going in for a business loan, and you don't have real property, large inventory or cash reserves, you're going to need an investor to guarantee the loan in exchange for your gold teeth and vital organs.

America has been sold on the idea that owning a business is a walk in the park and that all business owners are rolling in the dough. Nothing could be further from the truth. Operating a business is a daily challenge, interrupted by many sleepless nights, especially those night terrors brought on by your friendly neighborhood banker.

10

Don't Be a George, Part 1

Don't be a George.

I've used that term a lot over the years in working with salespeople. That's because I once worked with a guy named George who was raw and full of trepidation. He was a young man only a few years out of college. I was a bit older and more experienced, so we developed a natural mentor/apprentice relationship. We were working for a large, national billboard advertising company in Philadelphia and our job was to handle large, national advertising companies and advertising agencies that placed large, national advertising buys for large, national advertising companies. We were a team and our commissions and bonuses were dependent on each other's productivity. We either succeeded or failed together, so we were totally invested in each other's success — and all the good, the bad and the ugly that came along with such a symbiotic relationship. It was an interesting experience and, in the end, I probably learned a great deal more than George did, my curriculum being human nature and motivation.

And fear.

We wore suits to work every day back in that era of a more pronounced self-presence and heightened sense of professional identity. George drove a black, four-door Chevy Impala. It was big and roomy, as opposed to my smaller, Japanese gas-miser, so we usually drove his car when we were out in the field, tooling around the City of Brotherly Love, checking out billboard sites and giving the skeptical residents a heightened sense of the heebie-jeebies.

Because didn't we look like 5-0, rolling through the hood, carefully scrutinizing the landscape and scattering urban wolf packs in all manner and direction?

Fo shizzle m'prizzle.

Good times.

This was before the great emancipator of congenial social intercourse, before we were able to once and for all achieve mankind's great crawl to detached alienation from all that is not fallow, myopic and annoying. Yes, this was a time before the computer, when life moved along at a manageable pace and all you zombies showed your faces, a time before *Holy Father, what's the matter? Where have all your children gone? Sitting in the dark, living all by themselves.*

And speaking of hiding ...

One of the more unpopular jobs in the operation was spotting maps. When advertising companies or advertising agencies bought billboards, sometimes 200 or more at a time, they wanted to see where those billboards were located. So, as was standard operating procedure in the billboard industry, our art department created large facsimile maps of the market, and someone would methodically and tediously place red, numbered, self-adhesive dots showing where each of those billboards was located on the highways and byways of the greater Delaware Valley. This was time-consuming, detail-oriented clerical work that is now magically performed in seconds by the sophisticated wizardry of binary coded electronic circuitry in central processing units, humming and blinking away in the barren no-man's-land of don't-look-now-but-you're-a-superfluous-anachronism.

And guess who got to spot those maps. If you guessed the resented and misunderstood underbelly of a twisted corporate couture — the sales guys — you guessed right. And why not? Give it to those overpaid, expense account-abusing, golf-playing, booze-swilling, annoyingly upbeat, endorphin-addicted scene-stealers. What else do they have to do with their time? (Besides providing the revenue to pay everybody's salary and keep the company afloat, you mean?)

And guess which one of us, George or me, would like to pack up all his troubles in an old kit-bag and hunker down in the conference room for days on end with an X-Acto knife and magnifying glass, positioning all those little scarlet points of banality until his cornea screamed bloody murder.

Guess which one of us, George or me, preferred the safe haven of predictable monotony over the terror of rejection and personal devaluation. Guess which one of us would happily sit in a sequestered tomb of ersatz safety rather than risk the pain of failure in a world where failure is the norm and the only path to righteous success.

If you're having trouble deciding which one of us it is, here's a clue: The term we're talking about here is not "don't be a Rich."

Simply stated, George was more comfortable performing simple tasks that had a beginning, a middle and a neat, crisp ending, than sallying forth into the cave of the dragon to face the unknown and potential (expected?) pain of sales resistance and self-flagellation — a malady debilitating countless salespeople huddled in perceived security while the tides of opportunity rush all around them.

Sad but true.

This condition is the result of Fear Based Selling (FBS), where salespeople allow their actions to be dictated by fear and anxiety rather than focusing on the steps necessary to ensure success. It's a misguided but familiar route to take when confronting, especially for the first time, the reality of sales, that sales is hard. Really hard! Really, really hard, because most people say "no" and hurt your feelings.

Boo-freaking-hoo.

When it comes to selling successfully in the mean, cruel world, you better buck up, Buckaroo.

FBS is, unfortunately, the platform from which many salespeople and sales organizations operate, a position of defense and protection. When employed properly, FBS will ensure frustration, guilt and certain failure. So if it's failure you're after, and you find yourself constantly sharpening pencils, neatly stacking papers on your desk, organizing your sock drawer or performing other menial and unproductive tasks rather than making sales calls, don't stop. You're doing everything right.

Of course, if you want to go in a different direction and actually pursue success, don't be a George. And listen to The Hooters: *You don't have to hide anymore!*

11

Don't Be a George, Part 2

We don't do a lot of structured, formal sales training here. We focus more on real-world experience and field training — hands-on education, baptism by fire and all that," the congenial, relaxed and casually dressed young man told me. He went on to say that this company hires only experienced salespeople so it doesn't have to do a lot of time-consuming and expensive sales training, although it does give them thorough training on the features and benefits of the company's product line.

"Also," he added, "I'm not a big fan of sales theory or complicated, counterproductive sales systems."

"Neither am I," I said. "I am, however, a big fan of salespeople who know how to sell."

"Me, too," he gleefully responded, sitting up on the edge of his chair. "That's why I like to give my people enough room to grow on their own and figure out what works best for them."

"Sounds like you went to The School of Two Georges," I responded.

He looked clueless.

"Pickett and Custer," I added.

"Huh?"

Exactly.

I was meeting with the vice president of sales of a manufacturing company that employed about a dozen salespeople. I'd been invited to the meeting by the president of the company after he'd read an article I'd written on sales training. The president told me that sales had stagnated, and even declined a bit over the past couple of years, and he wanted me to meet with the VP and evaluate its sales program.

It was a short meeting — there wasn't much mystery involved in my investigation.

Surprisingly, this meeting was not an unusual one. Too many companies go to The School of Two Georges, favoring a *laissez-faire* approach to sales training over ... well, actual sales training. The School of Two Georges was founded in the names of George Pickett, famous for Pickett's Charge at Gettysburg, which pretty much determined the outcome of the Civil War, and George Custer, who got himself, two brothers, a nephew and a brother-in-law (along with 269 other poor souls) killed at The Battle of Little Big Horn. Pickett's Charge and Custer's Last Stand are two of the biggest debacles in American military history, engineered by men who eschewed book learning over field experience. And to prove their point, both graduated dead last in their classes at West Point.

At West Point, in mock deference to the Naval Academy's mascot, a goat is considered a lowly form of life. Ergo, the dubious title of "Goat" is conferred on the last cadet in line to receive his or her diploma, where Pickett and Custer accepted the honor enthusiastically, proclaiming to the world their shared obstinance and proclivity for myopic inspiration and guidance.

Just like so many dysfunctional sales organizations.

And not just companies, but individual salespeople as well. And the crazy part is, they invite me in to fix the problems, and then won't let me get close enough to help. It's mind-boggling and as frustrating as being the penultimate graduate at West Point and missing out on the bag full of cash that's donated by the other cadets and presented to the class Goat at graduation.

It reminds me of an experience I once had at the beach. It was late in the day and I was walking along the shoreline by myself, not far from our rented cottage, when I came across a young seagull tangled up in fishing line and trying to free himself from the intricate mess. He was obviously in a great deal of distress, with his wings pinned against his body and the line dangerously encircling his neck. He could move, but not very fast, so I was able to get within five or six feet of him. He looked up at me and even took a couple of tortured steps toward me in what I saw as a plea for help. I ran back to our cottage and grabbed a towel and a pair of scissors, then retrieved a pair of old work gloves from my car. My plan was to throw the towel over his head, hopefully producing a calming effect, and then hold onto him with one hand and cut the fishing line as quickly as I could with the other hand.

It wasn't a very good plan because he wouldn't let me get close enough to execute it. I tried for quite a while, but every time I threw the towel, he either moved or ducked his head. He really wanted — desperately needed — my help, and I wanted to help him. But he didn't trust me; he wouldn't let go of his fear and anxieties. He was slowly killing himself rather than accept help, like so many salespeople and sales forces who want and need help but aren't willing to go through the hard work and pain of confronting their inner demons and self-imposed obstacles in order to break out and fly free.

I know they need help and I know I can help them, but like the adage goes, you can lead a horse to water, but you can't make him drop out of The School of Two Georges, and in so doing, learn one of the most basic tenets of sales: DON'T BE A GEORGE!

Like my meeting with the VP of sales, my experience with that young seagull was disheartening. I finally had to call the beach patrol, who, in turn, called animal rescue, but I never found out the fate of that bird. That's too bad because I really wanted to save him, and maybe even take him home as a pet. But I know if I tried to drive him from New Jersey to Pennsylvania, with my luck, I would've been stopped and arrested for transporting an underage gull across state lines.

12

Don't Be a George, Part 3

Georgie Porgie, pudding and pie,
Kissed the girls and made them cry,
When the boys came out to play,
Georgie Porgie ran away.

I'm sure you remember this nursery rhyme from your childhood, but if you don't (and for your edification), it's a childhood nursery rhyme. In my ongoing mission for explicit accuracy, I've researched the origin of this rather interesting epigram thoroughly, and have come away completely confused (as usual). That's because (believe it or not) there are numerous scholarly opinions on its derivation. (And just how much time do we have on our hands?) Here's a sample from Wikipedia on the apparently inexhaustive enterprise to unravel this impenetrable mystery: "There is a further theory, equally unsubstantiated, but traditional in families which supported the Stuart line to the throne, that this is an old Jacobite rhyme that relates to the 1745 rebellion of mainly Scots. In this account the rhyme relates to King George II. It incorrectly implies that as the Jacobite army headed further and further south ('When the boys came out to play'), King George fled England for the safety of mainland Europe ('Georgie Porgie ran away'). Similarly, the convention of using 'ie' instead of 'y' or 'ey' at the end of words is prevalent in Scotland."

Got it?

On the other hand, I believe there's an obvious meaning to the poem that researchers are missing, one that should have smacked them square in the face: Georgie Porgie was a bad kisser. In today's invidious world where traditional boy/girl roles are being challenged from all directions, this quaint and seemingly harmless ditty is probably being purged from existence by the new crusaders for freedom of thought (as long as it conforms to accepted standards — set by guess who?) dedicated to stamping out all forms of frivolous, frolicsome, frisky fun. No, I don't believe the poem is about Georgie Porgie forcing himself on girls and making them cry; that would be an abhorrent theme for children in any era.

The 411 is that Georgie Porgie was clearly a wimp and not very good at kissing — that's what made the girls cry (and still does today) — and I'm guessing the reason he wasn't very good at it was because he never practiced. What? You never practiced kissing either? Bet you made some girls cry, too, huh?

I do know the territory. My first kiss came in the seventh grade with a girl named Babs who was all everything to me and most of the other boys in those simpler yet pubescently-confusing, restrictive and enervative days of hegemonized grammar school. We were sitting on the steps of her grandmother's attached apartment at the back of her house when the momentous occasion occurred — a primal shuffling of synapsed cross-sectoral neurotransmitters and mitochondria.

In other words, everything went kaplooey!

At that exact moment, my life turned upside down, because up until then, the only thing I wanted to do was play football. But now what? Could I play football and kiss girls? I wondered in a complete state of elated bewilderment: Football or kissing? Football and kissing? Football with kissing? No, that wouldn't work!

And along comes Franny in the eighth grade, a girl with a pure smile and a *mouth alive with juices like wine*. It was a few days before Christmas and I had bought her a cheap identification bracelet at Woolworths that was all the rage among us teenage Lotharios. Her name was engraved on its face, and when I gave it to her, she threw her arms around my neck and planted a smacker on me I have never forgotten (and never will). She had just burst into the room from outside, still wearing her stylish duffle coat, her skin cold and tingling to the touch, a sensation of hot and cold at the same time, a sweet taste of innocence with a faint hint of parsley mixed into all those exploding sensations pulsing through my body with that timeless exhilaration of hope and promise.

And unnerving as hell when Nell showed up in the ninth grade. A Sophia Loren look-alike with assets that were ... well, unnerving. (Do the words precocious or bodacious mean anything to you?) We were in the parlor of an old Victorian home at the private boarding school I'd been sentenced to for good behavior, innocuously (for the most part) sitting on a tufted, velvet love seat making out (yes, I had progressed to systemic kissing) when she stealthily slid her slippery tongue between my chaste lips and slithered it into my mouth.

Yuck!!!

I jumped up and ran out of the room.

"What the hell was that? Disgusting! Gross! Revolting!" my brain screamed.

"Hold on there," my emotions interrupted. "That was very interesting."

"Hubba, hubba!" from parts previously unknown but rapidly asserting a leadership role.

So, I persevered. I marched right back in there and continued the tutorial on my glorious quest to become a super-duper smoocher. And unlike The Fonz teaching Potsie and Ralph Malph how to kiss by having them do lip-ups on the side of a pinball machine, there's no substitute for placing lip to lip if you want to become proficient at the art of osculation. Just like in sales: If you want to become proficient at influencing people to buy your product or services, practicing your craft in a live format is the most effective way to improve your skill level.

Yes, we're talking about role-playing here, as many of you scamper off to safer spaces with your stomachs in knots and teeth chattering in a cacophony of agitated anxiety. The scourge of sales training everywhere, role-playing is the single hardest element of the process to get buy in. That's because most people are scared to death of laying it out there and opening themselves up to criticism. If you're one of the fainthearted legion of role-playing unenthusiasts, ask yourself a question: Would you rather have your prospects criticizing you to themselves as they continue to not do business with you, or subject yourself to the momentary prick of pain from your peers trying to help you get better?

It amazes me how many of my students develop illnesses when it's time to perform a role-play, or how many actually drop the course rather than play it out. It's much more than fear, folks, it's a phobia — a phobia of public speaking that, gone unchecked, will keep you shackled to the bench of never-reached-your-potential.

Brian Tracy writes at briantracy.com, "the average person ranks the fear of public speaking (also known as glossophobia) higher than the fear of death. The truth is, this fear could be hurting your professional and personal life. The fear of public speaking is very real. However, there are techniques to help you overcome your fears. There are even ways to help harness your energy in a positive way." The only way to do that is to work at it — take a proactive approach to your fear and conquer it, or at least harness it. And guess what? Role-playing in a comfortable group of friendly faces is an excellent place to begin. Additionally, there are myriad videos, books and articles (Tracy has a good one on his website) for overcoming glossophobia, but like everything else in life, it all starts with you taking the first step: Own the problem.

Don't be a George and hide from it, and listen to Paul

Hornung, who played for the Green Bay Packers and was my boyhood idol. He was my idol because of his preternatural ability to run down a football field with an oblong-shaped sphere tucked under his arm, and his preternatural ability to waltz through the night with gorgeously shaped blondes tucked under his arm. When asked how he was able to date so many beautiful women, old number five responded, "Practice, practice, practice!"

Or in the alternative, you can go with eminent psychiatrist Sidney Freedman: "Ladies and gentlemen, take my advice, pull down your pants and slide on the ice."

I don't know about you, but I'll take sustained success over a cold tush any day of the week — being a George is bad enough without that added degradation. Like how they taught us in grammar school to protect ourselves from nuclear attack, which we practiced as regularly as fire drills during those tempestuous Cold War days. We would be lined up in the hall and told to sit facing the wall, bring our knees up to our chests and put our hands on the backs of our heads. Then we were instructed to push our heads down between our legs as far as we could and hold them there for the duration of the drill.

I guess they thought a nuclear attack would be pretty much like an airplane crash. It wasn't until a few years later that I realized the position was developed primarily so that it would be easier to kiss our asses goodbye.

I mean, who wants a cold tush and cold lips — you'll make yourself cry, by George!

13

Ch-ch-ch-ch-changes
(turn and face the strange)

Hope and change.

That nifty, bedraggled homily may help you get elected in the overpromise-and-under-deliver world of politics (where disingenuous rhetoric is the currency), but in the world of business, there can be no hope for change unless you are willing to make changes.

And countless businesses aren't.

As unbelievable as that may sound, many businesses and businesspeople spend a great deal of time, money and energy trying to effect changes in their operation without making a commitment to making changes in the way they, or the folks running their operation, behave. The result is a roller coaster ride of "now you see it, now you don't" sleight-of-hand sorcery from the good folks who bring you all manner of cleverly disguised quackery and puffery.

Like weight-loss programs.

There is only one way to lose weight and keep it off: Change your behavior. If you want to get heathier and look and feel better, you need to reduce the amount of bad stuff you're putting into your body and increase your metabolism. In other words, eat less junk and get more exercise (and playing golf from a cart with a case of beer in the cooler doesn't count). But that takes work and discipline, which is much harder than grabbing a package of Twinkies and a bottle of chocolate Yoo-hoo.

That's why weight-loss is the forever No. 1 category in the

this-will-be-so-easy self-help industry, spawning such can't-miss (in making the author rich) programs like the Fat-Free Diet, the Low Carb Diet, the Grapefruit Diet, the Cabbage Diet, the 3-Day Diet, the 3-Hour Diet, the Liquid Diet, the Water Diet, the Sacred Heart Diet, the Lemonade Diet, the Hollywood Diet, the Beverly Hills Diet, the Tapeworm Diet, the Negative Calorie Diet, the Acai Berry Diet, the HCG Diet, the South Beach Diet, the Mediterranean Diet, the Zone Diet, the Detox Diet, the Macrobiotic Diet, the Perricone Diet, the Glycemic Index Diet and the Drop Dead and Lose Weight Diet, just to name a few.

Gimmicky, trendy parlor games to entertain and amaze and bring you back next time, salivating for the latest with the greatest, sure-fire, fit-into-a-size-six-that-is-really-a-size-12 hall of distorted mirrors, with lots of flashing bells and whistles and the slippery smell of snake oil seeping in through the floorboards.

And that's exactly what the good people mired and uninspired in the world of commerce do every day: Rather than commit to the hard work of making real change, they grab on to Johnny-come-lately and his magic carpet ride.

Enjoy the show, folks, and pay no attention to the man pulling the strings from above (or the hand picking your pocket).

When it comes to selling your product or service, there's no end to the myriad systems, strategies, methods and madness to capture those elusive butterflies of buy — tell-you-what-I'm-gonna-do and sign-on-the-dotted line, Clementine — sales programs designed to make you think you're doing something about your problems without the nasty business of actually having to deal with your problems.

As an example, in their international bestseller, *Blue Ocean Strategy*, W. Chan Kim and Renee Mauborgne write: "To fundamentally shift the strategy canvas of an industry, you must begin by reorienting your strategic focus from competitors to alternatives, and from customers to non-customers of an industry. As you shift your strategic focus from current competition to alternatives and non-consumers, you gain insight into how to redefine the problem the industry focuses on and thereby reconstruct buyer value elements that reside across industry boundaries."

Really?

In other words, you need to develop new customer bases and create new markets through product positioning and development, a simple concept masterfully illustrated in 256 pages of glorious fluff.

Look, folks, there are no esoteric tricks or secret formulas that can correct systemic problems, whether they exist in the entire organization or in a single individual who can affect the operation of making money. Unfortunately, we live in a world where we want and demand immediate answers and quick fixes, but there are none.

Never were, never will be.

If you need to make changes in order to grow or survive, there are five fundamental steps you should take:

Step 1 – Admit and own that you have a problem, or problems, that need to be fixed.

Step 2 – Identify the problem areas and isolate the root causes.

Step 3 – Create a plan to correct the problems.

Step 4 – Develop an action plan that assigns tasks and deadlines to individuals or teams.

Step 5 – Actually do the first four steps. Really.

Ha, ha! Right?

But it's no joke. I spend most of my time these days working with people who know it's not working, but aren't willing to admit that they, themselves, may be part of the problem.

It's maddening.

Bottom line: If you want to get better, you first have to accept that you need to get better and that cosmetic misdirections will not work.

Next, you have to put some diligence into discovering the

malfunctions that are preventing you from performing effectively. Then, arduously and comprehensively create a plan that addresses the core values you are trying to establish, and put in place a schedule for accomplishing those initiatives.

And then, of course, you have to do it — not just think about it or talk about it or dream about it; you just have to do it.

Otherwise, you'll be feasting on a wish sandwich. That's a sandwich where you have two pieces of bread and wish you had something in between.

Wishing and hoping won't bring change, nor will half-hearted efforts supported by bogus shamans. If you're not willing to change your behavior and be accountable for your actions, then you might as well play the lottery. Your chance of success will be better.

14

White Noise

The Artist Formerly Known as Prince is gone.

But not forgotten.

To the contrary, like his predecessors — Elvis Presley, John Lennon and Kurt Cobain, to name a few — death has only enhanced his popularity ... and cash flow, thanks to the always-unbridled media.

Back when it was still unusual and innovative to go by a single name, before every other would-be Cher who was looking to touch the sacred cloth of cool thought that being a hip, mononymous badass would help camouflage a conspicuous deficiency in the talent department, Prince was an interesting, gifted cultural icon. His songs were fun, his musical skills obvious and his persona mysterious and intriguing. I enjoyed his music immensely and we all boogied down to his hits in the latter part of the 20th century.

However, to devote several days for tributes, reminiscences and analysis to the purple rainmaker was a wee bit over the top, or as we like to say here in the 21st century, business as usual. The media were beside themselves over his sudden demise and rushed to program every tidbit and nuance of the life and times of Prince Rogers Nelson, gushing and sycophanting in excessive hyperbole.

But hey, *that's the way, uh-huh, uh-huh,* [we] *like it, uh-huh, uh-huh.*

Or more appropriately, that's the way the modern media fights their ratings wars and make money: by bashing us over the head repeatedly until we're practically comatose from the bombardment of relentless pandering.

Seems like they're *busy doing something close to nothing*.

As a result, we've become numbed to reasonable discourse, and it takes a Donald Trump blasting us with pomposity and bombast to cut through the clutter of tediously turgid and predictably puerile hullabaloo.

All that white noise.

Unfortunately for the status quo, the media and established politicians don't get it. They don't get it because they are the white noise — it would be like asking a fish to describe water. They are so flummoxed by Trump's success that they are beside themselves in exasperated indignation and frustrated puddles of melted hair gel. It's like fighting quicksand: The harder they rail against it, the further in they sink.

Without having a clue (not an uncommon position for many politicians and media types), they are the reason for Trump's popularity simply because he's not one of them, and the more they keep saying he's not one of them, the more people they drive to his side. Trump is poison ivy to a political system gone wild — a self-protected, privileged oligarchy that gave us a war of personal vengeance that won't go away and affordable health care that is anything but — and the more they scratch, the faster it spreads.

Because, love him or hate him, Trump has figured out how to beat the house.

Which is what you need to do if you hope to cut through all that pervasive white noise in today's business marketplace; you need to learn how to beat the old stall-and-hide technique that prospects have taken to new heights in this charming age of ubiquitous annoyance.

You know what I'm talking about: You call and call and call, but nobody calls you back. Or you finally get through and they smile, nodding their heads in agreement as you dazzle them with your magic tonic of super-salesmanship. They shake your hand and assure you they're very interested and will get back to you in a couple of days. Or they tell you to give them a call in a week after they've had a chance to discuss it with their partner, accountant, spouse, etc.

And then ...

You never hear from them again. They won't return your phone calls, won't answer your emails, won't respond to your texts and social media messages, won't even acknowledge that you exist. You're dead to them, or worse, you're a never was.

What a revoltin' development!

So how do you break through the clutter? How do you negotiate a path through the muck and mire? How do you rise above all that white noise?

How do you get prospects to pay attention to you?

It's not easy, and it's getting harder every day. With so many methods of contact — knocking on doors, phone calls, texts, emails, PMs, social media posts, snail mail — prospects are inundated with unsolicited solicitations to the point of being desensitized to almost all attempts.

But not all.

Which is good news to you progressive thinkers who are willing to adjust your sails to the wind, who will adopt a discipline of identifying opportunities and creating ways to capitalize on them. In the ongoing battle against the seemingly impenetrable walls of inaccessibility, there is hope for those willing to roll up their sleeves and work hard, for those intrepid few ready to step off the cliff of all that no longer works and leap into the churning currents of the new millennium. In today's professional environment, your success will be determined by an ability to make people notice you through a conscientious and imaginative effort of productive positioning.

Developing a plan and working on a discipline for combating the evolving mores of accepted business decorum are essential to your success and your well-being. I mean, how many slammed doors and ignored beseechments can a person stand before they start making ridiculously inconsistent and outrageous statements? How long before they start defying all logic and propriety and become intrusive and boorish and completely obstinate to the point of populist depravity?

Keep that up long enough and before you know it, you'll be qualified to run for president, where adversaries bellow at each other in a cacophony of discordant insults to the delight of all.

And *this is what it sounds like when doves cry.*

15

The 12 Days of Selling

On the first day of Christmas, my true love gave to me: A brand-new Apple iPad.

On the second day of Christmas, my true love gave to me: Two books on dragons and a brand-new Apple iPad.

On the third day of Christmas, my true love gave to me: Three shirts with French cuffs, two books on dragons and a brand-new Apple iPad.

On the fourth day of Christmas, my true love gave to me: Four calling buyers, three shirts with French cuffs, two books on dragons and a brand-new Apple iPad.

On the fifth day of Christmas, my true love gave to me: Five gold Cross pens, four calling buyers, three shirts with French cuffs, two books on dragons and a brand-new Apple iPad.

On the sixth day of Christmas, my true love gave to me: Six stripe-ed ties, five gold Cross pens, four calling buyers, three shirts with French cuffs, two books on dragons and a brand-new Apple iPad.

On the seventh day of Christmas, my true love gave to me: Seven finished call reports, six stripe-ed ties, five gold Cross pens, four calling buyers, three shirts with French cuffs, two books on dragons and a brand-new Apple iPad.

On the eighth day of Christmas, my true love gave to me: Eight sales assistants, seven finished call reports, six stripe-ed ties, five gold Cross pens, four calling buyers, three shirts with French cuffs, two hilarious books on dragons and a brand-new Apple iPad.

On the ninth day of Christmas, my true love gave to me: Nine paid expenses, eight sales assistants, seven finished call reports, six stripe-ed ties, five gold Cross pens, four calling buyers, three shirts with French cuffs, two hilarious, ridiculously insightful books on dragons and a brand-new Apple iPad.

On the 10th day of Christmas, my true love gave to me: 10 jobs delivered, nine paid expenses, eight sales assistants, seven finished call reports, six stripe-ed ties, five gold Cross pens, four calling buyers, three shirts with French cuffs, two hilarious, ridiculously insightful, reasonably priced books on dragons and a brand-new Apple iPad.

On the 11th day of Christmas, my true love gave to me: 11 prospects yessing, 10 jobs delivered, nine paid expenses, eight sales assistants, seven finished call reports, six stripe-ed ties, five gold Cross pens, four calling buyers, three shirts with French cuffs, two hilarious, ridiculously insightful, reasonably priced, last-word-on-sales books on dragons and a brand-new Apple iPad.

On the 12th day of Christmas, my true love gave to me: 12 sales a-closing, 11 prospects yessing, 10 jobs delivered, nine paid expenses, eight sales assistants, seven finished call reports, six stripe-ed ties, five gold Cross pens, four calling buyers, three shirts with French cuffs, two hilarious, ridiculously insightful, reasonably priced, last-word-on-sales, critically acclaimed books on dragons and a brand-new Apple iPad Pro with a 12.9-inch 2732 x 2048 resolution display, A9X processor, iPad Air 2-style design, four-speaker audio system, and a Smart Keyboard with an Apple Pencil all packaged in space-age Space Gray.

Phew!

16

The Business of Etiquette

I don't understand women.

I don't understand men all that well either, but I really don't understand women.

Especially when it comes to business etiquette.

I was at a trade show last week where I ran into a business acquaintance I hadn't seen for more than a year. We didn't have what you'd call a close relationship, yet when she saw me, she made a big fuss while negotiating through the crowded room.

I was caught off guard.

When we were in touching distance of each other, I started to stick out my hand, and she kind of leaned in toward me. I pulled my hand back and leaned in a bit toward her, slowly and indecisively bringing up my arms as she straightened her back and began to extend her hand. We froze for a moment, confused, and then awkwardly moved our bodies and arms in tentative, exploratory movements, not sure which way to go, reminiscent of a mongoose and a cobra squaring off, bobbing and weaving, looking for an opening, an opportunity to strike first before certain death, and in this case, of spastic embarrassment.

So, what's the story? When are you supposed to shake a woman's hand, give her a short, formal, stiff hug, squeeze her with an affectionate embrace, peck her on the cheek, kiss her on the lips, get a room?

I am very confused.

The rule of thumb used to be that a man waited for a

woman to extend her hand, and then he politely and gently shook it. Nobody hugged or kissed or made any other gesture of familiarity back when expressions of intimacy were discouraged in a business environment, except at the annual Christmas party where they were practically compulsory.

But we live in a more sensitive, touchy-feely world where outward, physical demonstrations of caring and compassion have replaced the burdensome task of actually having to care or be compassionate. It's all part of the speed and convenience of the computer age.

Instant karma.

And before it gets you ...

Here are a couple of tips on business etiquette in the new frontier:

Cell phones, right? Can't live with them, really can't live with them. You know, those devilish devices that some women carry in the back pocket of their expensive, skin-tight jeans that obviates the main function of expensive, skin-tight jeans; that handy umbilical cord ostensibly invented to make your life easier as it ominously becomes your life; those *Star Trek* precursors that enslave you in a virtual world as make-believe as *Star Trek*.

Yeah, those things.

Turn 'em off.

I know that sounds like blasphemy, but when you're with a client or prospect, it's bad form when the sinister little monster rears its ugly head. And not just the ringer, either. You can hear it vibrate and see those flashing lights when it goes off.

Yes, that's right: Turn it off completely and send a message that you're in the moment and fully engaged. Let your interlocutor know that she is the most important person in your life, right here, right now.

She will appreciate it, and you will reap the benefits of that gratitude.

And, as a residual benefit, your life will be much more pleasant, at least momentarily.

Then there's the time-honored and traditional ceremony of — cue the loud and booming echo chamber — THE EXCHANGE OF BUSINESS CARDS!

When you meet someone at a business function, you can start off on the wrong foot by asking, "What do you do?" Not only is this an indolent, ordinary approach, it can come off as rude and might be interpreted as a challenge. It's not a very good icebreaker and can set up your new acquaintance for responses like, "Not much" or "Anybody I can." Although those comebacks were real knee-slappers during the Hoover administration, they put you in the awkward position of having to force a laugh at the insufferably hackneyed gag line, and who wants to be in that kind of precarious position when trying to impress a potential buyer?

I prefer a more pragmatic approach. I like to introduce myself while handing over my business card. The recipient's normal response is to hand you his business card, which is a much smoother process than asking for it. When you receive the card, examine it carefully like it was the Dead Sea Scrolls, like it's the most interesting thing you've ever seen, and use it to organically start the conversation.

"Ah, Mr. Dormouse. I see you're head of security at the He-Who-Laughs-Last Casino. That must be a very interesting job."

The truth is, people like to talk about who they are and what they do, especially when the listener shows a genuine interest and hasn't put them on the defensive by forcing the issue with an impetuous and aggressive interrogation. If you want to effectively begin the process of gaining trust, make the other person comfortable; let him know he is important and that you enjoy being with him.

Like when you're having lunch and the check comes. Don't break off your conversation and grab it with a grandiose expression such as, "This is on me."

Of course it's on you. That's understood, and your superfluous reiteration of the obvious will come off as fishing for an acknowledgment and expression of gratitude.

Instead, maintain eye contact and stay focused on her and the conversation while you discreetly slide the check toward yourself. The message will be that she is the significant object of your interest and you are totally involved. Once the conversation winds down, look at the check quickly and pay it, but do not make any remarks like, "Wow! You had three martinis? Atta girl."

As you're leaving the restaurant, don't forget to hold the door. Old-fashioned manners never go out of style, and if you happen to be with a man, hold the door for him, too. Old-fashioned manners are gender-neutral, and you will never go wrong with a bit of civility and respect.

As far as shaking her hand or hugging her when you take leave of each other, you're on your own.

I haven't a clue.

17

Sailboats in the Desert

When I was a boy, my mom had a hard time waking me up in the morning, but not on Saturdays. On Saturdays I would pop out of bed at dawn, grab a bowl of Maypo and plant myself on the floor in front of the TV. There I'd sit for hours, mesmerized by anvils falling on unsuspecting heads, shotguns blasting holes through torsos, characters electrocuted, dismembered, tenderized, flambéed, shoved through meat grinders, drowned, thrown off cliffs, run over and smashed like bugs, impaled, suffocated, sliced, diced and grated.

A horror film festival?

Nope.

Saturday morning cartoons, a staple of every kid's weekend itinerary during the nascent era of remoteless, three-channels television. And in those golden olden days of the Road Runner, Bugs Bunny, Tom and Jerry and other various and sundry practitioners of witless violence and fatuous mayhem, life didn't get any better.

Now I get up on Saturday morning and go to the gym, the barber shop, the dry cleaner, the grocery store, and pursue other responsible, mundane activities of the mature and monotonous. But on a recent cold, wet, dreary Saturday morning, I eschewed my usual routine and lingered in bed to peruse the offerings of 21st century Saturday morning entertainment.

What a shock.

Gone were Fat Albert and The Banana Splits, replaced by local news and the insidious infection of cheap, easily available programming for hire: infomercials!

The modern-day incarnation of traveling medicine shows grabbed my attention with promises of an Adonis-like body and riches beyond my wildest dreams. Once again, I was captivated by the Svengali allure of Saturday morning's boob tube, only instead of Acme Corporation rockets and remarkably handy pitchforks, the weapons of choice were tight, Spandex shapeware and slicked-back hairdos that screamed "under no circumstances should you ever, ever trust me."

I didn't.

As I surfed up and down the channels, the two products that permeated the cableways were workout equipment and videos, and real estate programs, promising to make the tediously protracted and arduous processes of getting in shape and getting rich easy and accessible to anybody with a credit card at their fingertips.

One two three, oh that's how elementary it's gonna be.

The workout equipment and video programs demonstrated how much fun you would have losing that unwanted fat (as opposed to the wanted fat you'd prefer to keep) and building six-pack abs in 30 days or less. Imagine, years and ridiculous amounts of money building a body by Meghan Trainor, all gone in days with your new, sleek, state-of-the-art apparatus of enjoyable self-abuse that slides under the bed for easy storage — yours for only four convenient payments.

And if you want to know just how much fun they really are, go to any garage sale on Saturday morning instead of watching the Brother Love's Show. There you will find the same equipment, still practically brand new — hardly ever used — that you can have for only one convenient payment, usually about the price of a case of beer and a bag of chips.

And those real estate-to-riches mavens, boy, can they sling it. Forget The Donald going to the old man for a mill to get started, you can do it with your credit card. Just punch in the numbers and sign up for the class with no class for only several thousand dollars that you'll never see again.

Promise.

That's because buying and selling real estate is not easy, it's hard — very, very hard — and certainly not for the faint of heart. It's speculative and a huge gamble, and the can't-miss road to riches is littered with the lifeless bodies of the hopelessly ignorant, the folks who paid for the Shah of Sham's private jet.

It reminds me of an episode from *The Rockford Files* titled "The Great Blue Lake Land Development Company." In it, Jim Rockford gets caught up in the middle of a real estate swindle. His father, Rocky, says to him at one point, "No roads, no water, no electricity. They're selling an invisible lake.

"And that ain't all. Out there where there's nothing but sand and jack rabbits, this guy tried to sell me a boat.

"But they're doing business out there," Rocky continues. "These folks get to come out there and pry around and they see what they're getting for their money."

"No," Jim responds. "They see little white sails on a great blue lake, and barbecue every Saturday night at the club.

"It's called salesmanship, Rocky."

If you're selling people what they want, I guess that's one way to look at it. But selling something that the vast majority is never going to benefit from is not honest salesmanship, it's running a con game. If you want to be successful, sleep soundly and enjoy your life, you need to help people — recalling Zig Ziglar's words of wisdom: "You can have everything in life you want, if you will just help other people get what they want."

The ethical question in sales should not be, "Did it make money?" but "Did it help the buyer?" Another essential question to ask: "Did the sale benefit me or did the sale benefit the buyer?" A sale should benefit both parties, and that should be the goal of every salesperson.

The Saturday morning hucksters may very well believe in their products, but when they sell them as something they are not, or promise results that are never going to happen, then they are selling snake oil and should be tarred and feathered and run out of town on a rail, like in the good old days.

I'll take the good old days when my Saturday morning ritual was topped off by *Lunch with Soupy Sales*. After all, a pie in the face is better than a workout-induced hernia or a frozen pipe in a fool's-gold investment property in the next county at three in the morning during a snowstorm.

18

Rhinoceros? Imposerous!

Advertising is sales.

I've harped on that theme before, but then, I believe everything is sales.

In my first book, *From the Jaws of the Dragon: Sales Tales and Other Marginally Related Stuff,* I wrote, "... advertising is selling. Both fields of endeavor are based on the same principles, with the same expectations — to sell product."

Advertising, marketing, promotions, merchandising, they're all sales, only distinguishable by their different approaches to the same, basic discipline: *We gotta move these refrigerators; we gotta move these color TVs.*

I got a great deal of firsthand knowledge on that subject during a 35-year career selling advertising. In that time, I saw some ridiculous applications of David Ogilvy's basic tenet of advertising: sell, sell, sell. In *Confessions of an Advertising Man* (written circa *Mad Men*), Ogilvy schools his readers on the purpose of advertising: to sell product.

Period.

One of the axioms of effective advertising is to deliver the right message at the right time in the right place. So I was a bit baffled and amused when I recently came across a billboard for the protection of rhinoceri.

In Allentown, Pennsylvania.

Land of funnel cake, bulldog hood ornaments and geographically misplaced songs about rusting steel stacks.

But never to have had its bountiful topsoil trod by the thundering hooves of horned, odd-toed ungulates.

The ad showed a picture of a rhinoceros with copy that read, "I am not medicine. At least one rhino is killed every day due to the mistaken belief that rhino horn can cure cancer and hangovers. Stop wildlife crime. It's dead serious."

Hey, I'm the first guy to support any effort to help stamp out the insidious malignancy of hangovers, but according to the World Wildlife Fund (WWF), "There is no scientific proof of the medical value of rhino horn. Yet it is highly prized in traditional Asian medicine, where it is ground into a fine powder or manufactured into tablets as a treatment for a variety of illnesses."

Even more noteworthy, there are no rhinoceroses in Allentown, Pennsylvania, where the Asian population hovers around 2 percent and where there are no discernably defined Asian neighborhoods. There wasn't even a Chinese restaurant in the vicinity of the billboard.

Not to mention that both "black and white rhino populations are growing healthily overall," as reported by the WWF (which created the campaign). Accordingly, it appears that this ad is more of a preemptive strike since the WWF goes on to say that "continued poaching could see Africa's rhinos slide over the brink, into extinction."

You mean, if we keep indiscriminately killing a certain species of animal, it could disappear?

No kidding?

Like Cecil the lion?

Poor Cecil, we hardly knew ye.

But we do know all about your country of origin, Zimbabwe, where Mugabe troops indiscriminately use rape and other brutality against women in a violent strategy to hold power, not to mention a little genocide here and there. (Let's see some sanguine and pseudo-poignant meme on Facebook about that one, folks.)

But don't worry, Cecil, we've got your back.

(All right, before you send me nasty messages about animal rights, please know I have never killed a lion, a rhinoceros or any other of all God's creatures great and small, but not too small like the occasional mosquito I wantonly swat with no hesitation because, well, it's a mosquito. Also, the Christmas cards we send to our friends and family every year are from the WWF with pictures of cute wolves in peaceful, harmless serenity printed on recycled paper.)

And speaking of curious advertising, just when you thought it was safe to go back into football season, here comes a new batch of those creepy, disturbing DirectTV commercials that used to feature Rob Lowe playing loser alter-ego characters such as Less Attractive Rob Lowe and Scrawny Arms Rob Lowe. In today's popular style of nothing-is-ever-over-the-top-comedy where you are bludgeoned with sophomoric, marginally amusing bits until you lose all perspective, one of my favorites was Painfully Awkward Rob Lowe, who is shown standing at a men's room urinal unable to relieve himself because there are other people around.

Talk about uncontrollable guffaws.

Or how about the side-buster Total Deadbeat Rob Lowe who says, "My kids were always fighting over what to watch, but that's their stepdad's problem now."

Parental responsibility shirking.

Now let's be honest, does it get any funnier than that?

DirectTV claims the ads worked and helped sell product — a frightening insight into today's consumer. Luckily for those of us who still like our comedy to be, you know, funny, the Council of Better Business Bureau's National Advertising Division interceded over claims of misleading ad copy, shutting down the laugh factory.

Temporarily.

Because in comes Eli Manning and Tony Romo with their very own demented versions of the gag that refuses to die, proving once again that money talks, although not necessarily in a particularly humorous tone.

And speaking of creepy ads, the toilet paper industry has decided that decorum and taste are unequivocally antiquated virtues. First, we had Charmin featuring animated bears with toilet paper stuck to their behinds (which answers the age-old question, "Do bears use toilet paper in the woods?"), and now Cottonelle is touting commando-clean wipes.

Oh my, when will it all end?

No time soon, apparently.

Joe's Crab Shack is running a TV commercial showing a shrimp scurrying along going nowhere in some kind of aquarium on some kind of treadmill. Creepy doesn't begin to cover this one, as Jimmy Buffet is sure to be rethinking Margaritaville's afternoon snack. It's like McDonalds advertising a Big Mac while showing cows running from the slaughterhouse.

Or showing rhinoceroses basking in the mud while advertising sex aids. That's right, peeps, rhino tusks are also thought to be aphrodisiacs, which is preposterous.

I know.

I took six hits of that stuff one night and only three worked.

19

Who's the Boss?

I want to know something: Is there a reverse dress code at casinos that I'm not aware of?

All the lonely people, where do they all come from?

And speaking of expecting a big return on a small investment, I had breakfast at my favorite diner last week.

Winner, winner, chicken dinner.

(Fascinating fact: That quote is an amusingly clever bridge between casinos and eating cheap food. You may think it's from the movie *21*, or the TV show *Two and a Half Men*, or some other contemporary source, but years ago, Las Vegas casinos sold chicken dinners for $1.79. The standard bet back then was $2, so when you won, the dealer would shout out, "Winner, winner, chicken dinner." Stay tuned for more exciting vignettes of life in the fast lane.)

Anyway, I was by myself and in a hurry, so I sat at the counter. When the waitress (or server, if we must be politically correct, and who mustn't) brought my egg-whites, bacon and cheese omelet, I asked for an extra napkin or two (since I like to periodically wipe the counter of bits and pieces of dropped foodstuff and conduct other OCD-like cleansing tasks during my meal).

Regrettably, her attention was elsewhere and my request went unnoticed.

Several minutes later, she Road Runner'ed by, legs all atwirl, and asked if I needed anything. Once again, I asked for extra napkins, but she just smiled and left me in a cloud of metaphorical dust (while I looked up the number for the Acme

Corporation on my cell phone).

As I was mopping up my eggs, she came by carrying a tray full of dirty dishes and shot me a bleached blonde, teased and lacquered smile over her shoulder.

"You okay, hon?" she asked, but as I opened my mouth to speak, she barged through the swinging, stainless steel doors to the kitchen — gone with the wind.

And my extra napkins.

Lots of semisweet, pasteboard smiles, but no real attention to details or my needs.

Which got me thinking: Food servers could make a lot more money with a little sales training. Like everyone, they're in sales, selling themselves in order to get big tips — tips that can shrink or disappear right before their eyes if they don't pay attention to a few basic principles of the sales process.

The owner of the diner was at the cash register when I checked out, and I asked him if he ever thought of giving his waitstaff some sales training to learn to better serve his customers.

"That would be great," he said. "But they'd never go for it."

"Really?" I asked. "Even if you emphasized that it would help them make more money?"

"Unfortunately," he lamented, "they already think they know everything. I can't get them to do the simplest things around here, let alone put in extra time for training."

Gee, I guess the donuts are running the bakery.

It reminded me of an account I dealt with about a year ago. A woman had bought a hair salon and wanted to build up business. She told me she had worked at a shop years ago where the owners made the operators go through sales training, and it really helped. Business increased dramatically, and they all made more money. She was very excited and couldn't wait to get started.

However, when I called back the next week, she said they had decided to put it off for a few months. I was surprised, and when I asked why, she gave me the old stall about timing and establishing better comfort levels and Venus rising in the seventh house of the seventh moon.

And that was the last time I was able to get her to return my phone calls. Finally, I stopped in and confronted her.

"What happened?" I asked.

"Oh, we talked about it a lot," she said. "But, in the end, they really didn't want to do it."

"Do you want them to do it?" I responded.

"Why, yes," she replied. "But you know how it is. I don't want to upset my people."

"I understand completely," I said. "Perhaps you should consider leadership training."

"Oh yeah?" she mused. "Maybe, when the timing's improved and after we establish better comfort levels and Venus is rising in the seventh house of the seventh moon."

An associate tells me of a similar situation where he was pitching a company with a six-person sales staff that desperately needed sales training. He met with them a few times and eventually ran a seminar for the group to introduce the process. A few weeks later, the sales manager got back to him to say the group had decided not to go through with the training.

"Why?" he asked. "Don't you think the program has merit?"

"Of course. I like it and believe you could help us greatly."

"Then why aren't we doing it?" my friend asked.

"Because the salespeople don't want to do it," was the sales manager's mind-boggling answer.

Look, if you're making decisions based on employees' unwillingness to participate in programs that will strengthen them and help the company, then you have a serious problem.

Not with them — with you.

It's okay to be nice to your workers and treat them with dignity, but remember what Al Capone said: "You can get much farther with a kind word and a gun than you can with a kind word alone."

So step up and do the right thing: be the boss. Make

decisions based on what's best for the organization and assert yourself to make it happen. Otherwise, it won't be long before you'll be hearing:

Loser, loser, big bamboozler.

20

I'm Late, I'm Late, for a
Very Important Date!

I was drafted three times during the Vietnam War, but never served.

Why, you may ask?

It wasn't because I was unpatriotic or anti-military or even opposed to the Vietnam War, per se.

It was because I was afraid of getting killed.

My high school friends, returning home from their tours of duty, scared the daylights out of me with tales of mayhem and the incomprehensible destruction of property and life. I already knew something about the seemingly futile carnage from news reports and because a football buddy was killed after being in-country for only three days, senselessly terminated with extreme prejudice by friendly fire — the result of an artillery miscalculation by another 19-year-old who was too young to buy a drink back home.

I had a brother at Khe Sanh, fighting off the Viet Cong. They're still there, he's all gone.

My Johnny-come-demoralized-and-limping-home friends sternly advised me not to go, at any cost. I took their advice and legally avoided induction — three times.

Twenty-some years later, after the war's memorial was built in Washington, D.C., and *Platoon* had been released, Vietnam vets were finally getting the positive recognition they deserved, and some of my old friends, who had two decades of pent-up anger, confronted me with, "Where were you?" It was more of an accusation than a question, and I would meekly answer, "I listened to you."

Life is full of ironies.

Like the first time I got drafted.

I was to report to my Selective Service Center at 7 a.m., but being a sufferer of chronically-late-syndrome, I didn't arrive until around 7:20. There were two buses lined up in front of the building to take us to Philadelphia for physicals and swearing-in. When I finally showed up, a sharp-looking guy with sergeant stripes on his sleeves told me to get on the second bus.

"I missed the first bus, huh?" I joked.

"That's for Marines," he replied.

"Marines? I thought the draft was for the Army."

"For guys like you — scruffy stragglers — it is," he scoffed. "The ones who were here early get to be Marines. The Marines want the best, the Army gets the rest."

"I take it you're a Marine," I smirked.

"Get on the bus, dogface!" Only he didn't use the suffix "face" — he used a different word that is usually associated with a byproduct of the other end of the anatomy. And with that short but sweet elegy, my fleeting chance to be one of the few, the proud, rumbled off in front of me, carrying my peers to exotic places like Parris Island, Huế and Hill 861. I, on the other hand, was given a six-month deferment after failing the physical and ordered to see an Army orthopedic specialist. He would, I was told, diagnose what effect the major reconstructive shoulder surgery I'd had a couple of years earlier would have on my ability to obliterate other human beings.

As I was getting back on the bus to head home from Philly, the same sergeant who had greeted me that morning told me I was very lucky. "The Marines wouldn't go for that old football injury crap," he said. "They would have passed you, boy, and you would have been mine."

Thank heaven for my chronically-late-syndrome.

I try to be on time, I really do. As a matter of fact, every year when I list my goals, "make an effort to be on time" is always right near the top. But *when logic and proportion have fallen sloppy dead,* I'm once again captivated by the wise words of William Faulkner in describing a father giving his son a watch that's a family heirloom (from *The Sound and the Fury*): "... I give you this mausoleum of all hope and desire; it's rather excruciatingly apt that you will use it to gain the *reducto adsurdum* of all human experience ... I give it to you not that you may remember time, but that you might forget it now and then for a moment and not spend all your breath trying to conquer it."

And that's all I'm trying to do: avoid *reducto adsurdum,* and not be a prisoner to time.

I'm sure you've heard the old chestnut that if you're 15 minutes early, you're on time, and if you're on time, you're late. (You ever wonder who makes up that drivel? My old Marine sergeant buddy?) In the end, though, all you have are 15 minutes lost.

Look, it's simple math: Let's say you have five events a day — appointments, meetings, conferences, dates for lunch, coffee or drinks, whatever — and you arrive 15 minutes early for each one: that's an hour and a quarter every day! I don't have that kind of time. I could make another sales call or two in an hour and a quarter. And as another old chestnut goes, time is money.

They're stealing your money, man.

It's been my experience that a fixation on punctuality is often a straw dog, constructed to deflect attention away from other systemic inequities. Like a company I worked with recently that would get all bent out of shape if I was a few minutes late, but had no problem canceling appointments with little or no notice, and interrupting our meetings for phone calls or to take care of other business. What was good for the goose was apparently not so good for the gander.

You'd think they would have gotten used to my chronic tardiness and made adjustments, like we do for our annual family Christmas party — one couple always arrives early, and another always arrives late. If the party's at 7 p.m., we tell the compulsively early-arrivers it starts at 7:30, we tell the habitual-latecomers it starts at 6:30, and everybody gets there at about the same time.

Piece-a-cake.

Truth be told, given my predilection for being fashionably late, I'd prefer to do business in New York City and Los Angeles. In New York, you're expected to be late because of the difficulty in getting around town, and in L.A., nobody cares. These are the mellow folks who leave Dodger Stadium after the sixth inning with the score tied zero-zero and both pitchers throwing no-hitters. Not much moves their needle, unless it's a bitchin' dune buggy ride up in the hills or a few gnarly waves off The Wedge at Newport Beach.

Folks of the customarily condemnatory clan who delight in monitoring other people's behavior say chronically late syndrome is symptomatic of laziness, shows a profound disrespect of others, is irresponsible, indicates a self-centered personality and is a bellwether for a lot of other nefarious attributes. I'm not saying there's anything wrong with being on time; in the big scheme of things, it's a desirable characteristic to possess, but does not necessarily make you a good person. By the same token, being late does not indicate a tendency toward an immoral and imprudent temperament.

To the contrary, businessinsider.com says, "People who always run late are more successful and creative."

See!

And it's not our fault. Diana DeLonzor, author of *Never Be Late Again*, writes, "Most late people have been late all their life, and they are late for every type of activity — good or bad ... some experts subscribe to the theory that certain people are hardwired to be late and that part of the problem may be embedded deep in the lobes of the brain."

Better yet, we are eternally optimistic, according to John Haltiwanger, senior politics writer at Elite Daily: "People who are continuously late are actually just more optimistic. They believe they can fit more tasks into a limited amount of time.

Simply put, they're fundamentally hopeful. Researchers have found optimism has a myriad of physical health benefits, from reducing stress and diminishing the risk of cardiovascular disease to strengthening your immune system."

Isabella Eckett, assistant editor at Talent Sales Manager, adds, "People who are late have a greater inability to feel stressed, leading to health benefits, but also think outside the box and look at the bigger picture. All of these things lead to greater success at work, alongside a longer life."

So there, all you judgmental devotees of *reducto adsurdum!*

If you still don't believe there are myriad benefits to being late, just ask J.P. Morgan, the legendary financier who helped build the industrial revolution. He had a personal suite with his own private promenade deck and a bathtub equipped with a specially designed cigar holder on a luxury liner sailing from Southampton, England, to New York City, but missed the departure because he lingered to enjoy his morning massage and sulfur bath. Distraught, he was left standing on the dock, watching the three functional and one decorative smokestacks of the Titanic fade into the horizon.

21

Saturday Bloody Saturday

While in high school, I had a part-time job working at a slaughterhouse on Saturday mornings. The place was kosher and closed on the Sabbath, so I pretty much had the whole compound to myself. One of my jobs was to clean the offices: empty the trash cans, dust a bit and mop the floors. There was a fairly sophisticated (for the times) PA system that I could connect to the radio, so I'd dial in WIBG, or Wibbage, out of Philadelphia and rock down to big-boss hits like *Wooly Bully* and *She's About a Mover* while dancing around the offices with my mop. I enjoyed the mindless routine after spending a week in pre-enlightenment lockdown, studying isosceles triangles and the periodic table and learning (rather painfully) that deportment and strict adherence to rules trumped intellect and creativity.

I loved that job.

Until the end of my shift when I had to shovel the blood.

Jewish law dictates that the animal's blood must be washed and removed from the carcass in a rather complicated process before it can be declared kosher. After that ancient procedure was performed, the blood, bones and other remnants of the recently deceased ended up in a big oven where the blood was dried into a fine, rust-colored powder that was used for fertilizer. The finished product was called blood meal, and to a teenage boy focused on filling the tank of his '57 Chevy so he could drive it to the levee with Betty Sue pressing up oh-so-next to him on the front bench seat of his super-cool, SoCal ride, it was disgusting but expedient for acquiring said petroleum byproduct.

My job was to shovel the pile of animal-blood powder into burlap bags so it could be loaded onto a truck and shipped to a nearby vegetable farm that was a favorite with the first wave of long-haired, leather-festooned vegetarians. This was in the days before OSHA, so I wore no goggles, no facemask or any other kind of protection against the insidiously pervasive, erstwhile dust-of-life. I breathed in the revolting, nauseating stuff as it invaded my eyes, ears and nose, and got all over my clothes and work boots.

It was a gross mess.

After a few months on the job, the owner of the company showed up one morning and, for a few minutes, watched me shovel the repulsive bovine soot. Finally, he came up to me and said, "You know, you're the first boy I've hired to make it past two months. You do a nice job. I'm giving you a raise."

Yay!

I went from a dollar an hour to a dollar-10, still 15 cents below the minimum wage of the day. But that was an extra 40 cents a week, and after taxes, bought a gallon of gasoline and more time snuggling up to Betty Sue, so I was a happy blood-shoveler that day.

I was reminded of that story recently while conducting a sales workshop on prospecting. We were discussing the problem of meeting decision-makers in the new frontier of ubiquitous electronic intrusion, where ducking sales folk has become a major component of running any business. I was saying that the traditional process of cold calling has become somewhat obsolete; that telephoning or knocking on doors unannounced is a huge waste of valuable time; that in this day and age of powerful computers and cell phones, you can research an account in depth before trying to make contact. I was explaining how you can learn volumes about a particular business and its people by Googling them, digging through their websites, visiting their Facebook and LinkedIn pages, and investigating other sources to learn more about their interests and habits and narrow the time spent chasing an army of red herrings.

At that point, a member of the group said, "Yeah, but that's a lot of hard work."

"Shoveling blood is hard work," I blurted before even thinking about what I was saying. "Doing preparation and research on an account is a walk in the park compared to shoveling blood. Not to mention, all success is predicated on hard work."

In workshops and in coaching individual salespeople, I've learned that it's not just laziness or lack of motivation that keeps salespeople from succeeding: it's also fear — fear of failure. It's safer and easier to keep calling on the same old prospects over and over again, even though the possibility of getting any business is extremely low, than it is to take the risk of pursuing the unknown and facing full-frontal rejection.

That's hard.

It's one thing to be persistent on an account that has real potential, but quite another to hide behind old, dog-eared leads that will never turn into business, but keep bringing you back to the safe Land of Mights and Maybes. Okay, I know it makes sense to pick the low-hanging fruit first, but when those easy pickings are gone, you can either spend your limited time rummaging through the rotting, insect-infested droppings on the ground, or get a ladder and start climbing.

Or grab a shovel and start shoveling.

Sure, it's much harder to work from a ladder, and there's always the threat of falling off, but as any young boy who spent a summer picking peaches can tell you (and yes, I did that, too), the tastiest, juiciest fruit is at the top of the tree.

I had a lot of interesting jobs growing up, and I was lucky to learn early on in life that hard work has its rewards, like the chance for a brief reprieve from the ordeal of spending seven hours a day in the involuntary institutional confines of higher education, and giving me a little time to bebop with my mop and contemplate the more important stuff in life — like what exactly did Bobbie Gentry and Billie Joe McAllister throw off the Tallahatchie Bridge.

22

All the Wrong Junk in All the Wrong Places

So Charlie Sheen is HIV-positive and wants us to know he's a new man because of it.

Oh. Okay.

He revealed his condition to Matt Lauer on *Today*, where he said, "It's a hard three letters to absorb. It's a turning point in one's life."

My question is: whose life has reached the turning point? Based on body language, it doesn't appear to be Good Ol' Swingin' Charlie's.

During the less-than-momentous (nor surprising) pronouncement, he bobbed and weaved and stuttered and squirmed and squinted and darted his eyes all over the place, creating the impression of a disingenuous and insecure little boy sitting in the principal's office. Or worse, a manipulative act, staged and orchestrated for the salivating masses waiting to lap up every crumb of vicarious bad-boy misadventure.

Sheen's mouth was saying one thing while his body language spoke much louder with a very different message. He would lean forward on cue with a look of sincerity when making a point (like a trained actor?), and after he had delivered the line, slouch back in his chair in an "I don't give a tinker's damn about any of this" posture. It was quite a show with conflicting and colliding messages galore. Unfortunately for The New Charlie, body language trumps the spoken word every time.

And by a huge margin, according to research conducted at

the University of Pennsylvania, where we learned that communication is made up of 70 percent body language, 23 percent tonality and only 7 percent the spoken word.

Poor Charlie, trying hard to sell his ostensibly cleaned-up persona while the body he spent decades abusing betrays him in the clutch.

Seems fair

But at least he made an effort to pretend to care, which is more than I can say for Sam Donaldson. As you may recall, Donaldson, who is probably best remembered as being President Ronald Reagan's nemesis, was a reporter, anchor and commentator for ABC News back in the days when Charlie was just taking off the training wheels on hedonism and debauchery.

In 1986, Reagan gave a commencement speech at Glassboro High School, and Donaldson, along with the usual throng of media, accompanied the president on his trip to South Jersey. Now imagine, this is graduation night for the senior class, excited with anticipation of a momentous evening — the biggest night in their young and unsophisticated lives, highlighted with a speech by the president of the United States of America.

Wow!

And in walks Donaldson — in front of the graduating class, its parents, grandparents, teachers, administrators and all of America watching on national TV — slouched and painfully disinterested, a smirk of obvious contempt for the entire proceedings on his face, his tie askew and resembling somebody on his way to the dentist for a root canal.

His body language screamed: I am better than all of you and my life is so much more important than yours, you bunch of losers.

Geez, couldn't the guy have shown a little respect, maybe hitch up his tie and force a smile, any act of kindness for the students about to take a walk they've dreamed of for years?

That short stroll of Donaldson's told you all you ever

needed to know about the man, and none of it good; a precursor to the coming wave of narcissistic journalists who care more about their Q-Ratings than truth, justice and the American way, all foretold in Donaldson's loutish, sanctimonious body language.

Such is the power of the unspoken word.

In an altruistic attempt to prevent you from ending up like the two aforementioned schmucks (which I'm pretty sure I'm allowed to say now that Donald Trump has introduced dirty Yiddish-like insults to the lexicon), here are a few tips:

Never cross your legs in a meeting unless you really, really need to evacuate your bladder. Crossing your legs can be perceived as a sign of weakness (especially if it's because of that bladder thing), but if you must, be careful where you point your crossed foot. If you point it at your listener, it sends a message of subservience and puts her in a position of control. If you point it toward the door, it may be interpreted as a lack of respect and a desire to flee. If you point it toward yourself, see an orthopedist immediately.

Avoid crossing your arms even if you're very cold and you'd prefer to keep that knowledge to yourself. Crossing your arms can be perceived as defensive or indifferent, or having a sense of superiority, or displeasure, or acceptance, or familiarity, or, according to the 3 million-plus body language sites on the internet, every other emotion in the entire range of the human experience. So as not to confuse your audience, and to be safe, avoid crossing any and all body parts ... especially your eyes.

According to Zig Ziglar (and every other biped, carbon-based life form with the ability to extrapolate), the eyes are the windows to the soul. According to the 3 million-plus body language sites, what you do with your eyes can reveal every hidden and repressed secret within your psyche, if interpreted by a trained expert.

If you look up, you're a thinker and creative. If you look down, you're insecure and a liar. If you look sideways, you're avoiding confrontation and the truth. And if you look in any other direction, you're Jar Jar Binks.

My advice is to wear sunglasses — just tell them your *future's so bright,* [you] *gotta wear shades.*

I can't believe Charlie Sheen didn't think of that. Of course, his ability to extrapolate most likely involves leather, latex and Mazola Corn Oil, and the glasses probably would just keep slipping off his face.

Now that's some body language Matt Lauer could use for his Q-Rating.

23

Of Profiles, Roles and Pigeonholes, Part 1

Pinky rings.

Pinky rings and pipes.

Pinky rings and pipes and bow ties.

All very bad medicine.

As I was coming up through the ranks, various characters of dubious ethical orientation would give me advice on what to look for in a prospect that might provide some insight into personality, disposition, trustfulness, decisiveness or favorite dance steps — telltale signs, for sure, that would prevent me from wasting time or applying an ineffective methodology or using the wrong moves.

One two, cha cha cha.

My first sales manager told me never to trust anybody wearing a pinky ring. As he put it, "Only one finger was intended to wear a ring, and they named it the ring finger. Get it? Unless you're a drummer for The Beatles, it's the only finger appropriate for a ring. People who wear pinky rings do so for a reason — they're covering up. It's all subterfuge.

"Did you ever notice how they're always waving those things around, right under your nose so you can't miss them? Talk about sleight-of-hand: You concentrate on the pretty, shiny bauble and never see the larceny.

"Pinky rings are tools of the devil — avoid them like the plague," he concluded, emphatically, pounding the desk in front of him.

And that advice stayed with me all these years: I never wore a pinky ring.

God forbid.

Then some time later, I worked for a guy who hated pipe smokers. I don't know why — maybe his Uncle Ernie smoked a pipe — but he told me to never do business with a pipe smoker.

"They're incapable of making a decision," he said. "They're the biggest time-wasters out there. Pipe smokers always want to be part of the conversation, even though they never have anything important to say," he continued. "They use that pipe like a weapon, pointing it at you in a gesture of intellectual profundity, while it emanates from a vacuous cavern of moldy, ineffectual meandering and directionless posturing.

"They'll try to engage you in an empty discourse of irrelevance with lots of smoke and mirrors," he said. "But in the end, they cannot make a decision — it's infuriating! Mark my words and avoid them like the plague!"

And yet another vehement warning of potential catastrophe and mayhem.

Okay, okay, okay: I'm getting married and I want to learn how to tie a bow tie so I can wear a real bow tie with my tux at the pending nuptials. I'm with a co-worker in the 35th floor men's room of the glass and steel edifice poking out of the midtown Manhattan skyline like another match in a matchbook, where we work for a large international media company. My co-worker, Mickey, *a man of wealth and taste*, is a product of fine breeding, and, most importantly, he knows how to tie a bow tie.

As Mickey is taking me, step by step, through the arcane and inexplicable alchemy of bow tie tying, in walks the CEO of the company, a man of few words but much stern condemnation. He immediately sees us standing in front of the mirror, colorful ribbons of imported silk in our hands, with looks on our faces like we just got caught hopping over the back fence, and he laughs.

"Bow ties," he says. "Boy, do I hate bow ties."

"Why's that?" I ask, relieved at not being silently, yet sternly condemned.

"People who wear bow ties are insufferable; they're smug, condescending fools. They think they're better than everybody else. And it's no act or overcompensation. They really believe they're superior beings. They are impossible to deal with because they are convinced that they are always right.

"I don't like doing business with any self-righteous, self-absorbed, bow tie-wearing fancy-pants, and you should avoid them like the plague."

And that was that — add bow ties to list of banned eccentricities.

Bada bing.

I must admit, over the years, I have not stayed ever vigilant against the insidious, subliminal influence of pinky rings, pipes and bowties, in spite of my bizarro-mentors' droll caveats. I have, however, been plagued by the plague, or at least the selling thereof.

Chuckle, chuckle.

The truth is, if you want to be successful in sales (or life), you can't, nor should you, avoid any particular personal characteristics, mannerisms or singular manifestations of individuality. People are people, and as The Doors once proclaimed as Jim Morrison slipped into a nice, hot bath in Paris, "People are strange."

The key is to embrace that strangeness, to celebrate those peculiar idiosyncrasies that we all have in order to build a bridge between you and your prospect. It's the only way she's ever going to let you into her world, and until she does that, you're going to be seeing *faces come out of the rain,* where *no one remembers your name.*

You can't judge a person based on one characteristic, or even a predetermined set of characteristics. In the long run (the long run to the bank, that is), it doesn't work, and if you try to operate within such narrowly defined parameters, that long run will continue to get longer and longer.

Like a guy I worked for a while back.

My first day on the job, he called me into his office and lectured me for about an hour on my shoes. The gist of his cautionary advice was that he was going to keep his eyes on my shoes to make sure they were stylish, clean and polished. He assured me he would know how I was doing by the condition of my footwear.

Over time, as I got to know him better, I came to realize that my first impression of him — that he was a complete moron — was inaccurate. No, he was much more than a complete moron. He was also shifty and untrustworthy, he would never make a commitment, he spent all his time covering his backside and he was aloof and sanctimonious.

Of course, he wore a pinky ring, smoked a pipe and was always in a bow tie.

So maybe shoes were an accurate barometer.

Who knew?

24

Of Profiles, Roles and Pigeonholes, Part 2

Mirror, mirror on the wall, who's the fairest of them all?

It certainly wasn't Sylvia Plath, who apparently wasn't crazy about mirrors. In her poem *Mirror* she wrote:

> *I am silver and exact. I have no preconceptions.*
> *Whatever I see I swallow immediately*
> *Just as it is, unmisted by love or dislike.*
> *I am not cruel, only truthful —*
> *The eye of a little god, four-cornered.*

The poem is written from the mirror's perspective and describes the woman who uses it:

> *I am important to her. She comes and goes.*
> *Each morning it is her face that replaces the darkness.*
> *In me she has drowned a young girl, and in me an old woman*
> *Rises toward her day after day, like a terrible fish.*

I first read that poem while in college, and the image of a terrible fish rising out of the mirror has stuck with me, a constant reminder that *time flies over us, but leaves its shadow behind*. That terrible fish awaits us all, patiently mirroring *every breath you take, every move you make, every bond you break, every step you take,* [it'll] *be watching you.*

So it was with mild amusement that I entered the world of sales and was introduced to the concept of mirroring. That was many years ago when the accepted and expected style of selling was hard, fast and cold — get in there, do most of the talking, dazzle them with your fancy footwork, get the sig and get the hell out.

Quickly, before they realize what hit them.

Fortunately, in most sales offices, that anachronistic type of high-pressure selling has been replaced with a much more cooperative, supportive approach. It had to be — people became too educated and sophisticated for that kind of bulldozing. Most of those pushy, forceful methods have been jettisoned, but mirroring resolutely refused to relinquish the rather ridiculously obsolete *modus operandi* of obtrusive manipulation.

Mirroring, in its natural form, is inherent and intuitive in the human condition; it is the subconscious replication of another person's physical and nonverbal behavior. Mirroring takes place in everyday interactions, and often goes unnoticed by the person enacting the mirroring as well as the individual who is being mirrored. The activation of mirror neurons within an individual starts the process, and, as a result, allows a greater connection to, and understanding of the individual being mirrored. In turn, it gives the subject of the mirroring a comfortable connection to the mirrorer, and a rapport begins to develop. Mirroring is different from imitation because imitation is a conscious and overt effort to copy another person, while mirroring is often covert and subliminal.

Mirroring can take the form of dress, mannerisms, body language, vocabulary and speech patterns. In most cases, it works on a subconscious level and is why people who spend a great deal of time together start to look and sound alike. When we meet someone whom we want to get to know or have a relationship with, we automatically emphasize in our own behavior their most prominent characteristics. It's a reflex action to put them at ease and help build trust.

This science has been around a long time, so it wasn't surprising that the rapacious 20th century boys of covetous inspiration seized upon the concept to further their pursuit of all that sparkles and shines. They believed you can quickly develop rapport with a customer by consciously mirroring their behavior. For example, if the customer sits down and crosses her legs, you cross your legs; if he leans back in his chair, you lean back in yours; if she speaks slowly, you speak slowly; and so forth. The hope is that it sends a positive message, and, in some manner of convoluted chicanery, shows that you are paying respect. The logic then follows that your flattering behavior will make the prospect feel important and signal that you're one of the good ones.

The whole notion is patently absurd and the province of purveyors of serpent lubricant. Aggressive folks don't want to be confronted with other aggressive folks, and the meek want and need someone who can be a bit assertive. But what people want most of all is for you to be yourself so they can decide if they want to do business with you.

When I find myself sitting across the desk from a salesperson trained in mirroring, I like to have a little fun. I cross my legs and after they follow, I sit up straight and then lean forward. When they comply, I lean back in my chair, and the more they mirror me, the quicker I go until they become completely distracted and baffled. It's quite amusing to watch.

If you want to be successful dealing with other people, the only mirror you should be consciously looking at is the one showing your own reflection, because the only way people will like and trust you is if you like and trust yourself first. Learning a manipulative technique isn't going to get you there, brothers and sisters.

It's a ruse, just like the opening line in this chapter.

Although most people believe that those words are what the vain, evil queen in *Snow White* said, the actual line is, "Magic Mirror, on the wall, who, now, is the fairest one of all?" So even if you can find a magic mirror to try to create your own reality, the mirror known as real life never lies, and like poor Sylvia's terrible fish, is always there, always following *every move you make, every vow you break, every smile you fake, every claim you stake,* [it'll] *be watching you.*

25

Of Profiles, Roles and Pigeonholes, Part 3

When I first got into sales, a grizzled old veteran pulled me aside, put his arm around my shoulder and in a conspiratorial whisper told me that if I wanted to be a successful salesman, I had to be sincere, and once I could feign that, I'd make a lot of money.

True dat.

As I was taught over the next few decades, pretending to be something I was not would make people like and trust me: Watch how they act, look for clues, mimic their behavior, *do this, don't do that, can't you read the sign?*

After all, imitation is the sincerest form of flattery, right?

Reminds me of a scene from *Beetlejuice,* a movie made back when Michael Keaton truly could soar. In it, Beetlejuice (Michael Keaton) is trying to close a deal with the Maitlands (played by Alec Baldwin and Geena Davis), ghosts who are trying to rid their home of an annoying family from New York City named the Deetzes.

"I'm the ghost with the most, babe," is how Beetlejuice describes himself while trying to seduce Lydia, the Deetzes' lugubrious daughter.

Beetlejuice is billed as a freelance bio-exorcist who claims he can chase away the living. In an attempt to sell his services, he affects a persona of similar disposition and taste to the innocent and unsuspecting Maitlands, miraculously aping Adam Maitland's clothing.

"Don't go yet," he pleads. "Come on, we're simpatico. Look at us. We shop at the same store ... we're like peas in a pod.

"You want someone out of the house. I want to get someone out of your house.

"You've been to Saturn. I've been to Saturn!

"Whoa. Sandworms. You hate 'em, right? I hate 'em myself.

"Kids, what do I have to do to strike a deal with you two?"

The Maitlands see through the charade and reject the crafty tactic as Beetlejuice gives it one last shot: "Hey! You've got to work with me here. I'm just trying to cut a deal. What do you want me to do? You bunch of losers! You're working with a professional here!"

Oh yeah, a professional, circa 20th century forgettaboutit, complete with disingenuous, high-pressure arm-twisting, devious misdirection and emotionally manipulative bullying and coercion.

Just the way I learned it.

And the way many dinosaurs still teach it.

Not too long ago, I attended an event conducted by a guy from an internationally known sales training company. The subject of his talk was learning styles and how recognizing them can lead to more sales. According to him, most people possess a dominant or preferred learning style, as defined by cloistered, insulated behavioral scientists who specialize in profiles, roles and pigeonholes (and who may occasionally have to create one or two in order to support predetermined conclusions). According to the leading experts in white elephant preservation, those styles can be classified into three basic categories: visual learners, auditory learners and kinesthetic learners.

In a nutshell (and not necessarily the same one those rigid compartmentalizers escaped from), visual learners acquire information by seeing it, auditory learners by hearing it and kinesthetic learners by feeling it.

The trainer explained that by studying the characteristics of a prospect and using techniques to exploit that style (techniques he'd be happy to teach for a price), you can surreptitiously acquire an advantage that will help you gain trust and create confidence. He said we needed to be like psychologists and figure out how people's minds work so that we can influence them to buy our products. In other words, learn lots of cool parlor-tricks to discover their vulnerabilities and then prey on those exposed predispositions and weaknesses.

Good plan, Attila.

The problem is that the discipline it's based on is a myth. It's nearly impossible to identify these narrowly defined types of learners because most people have mixed or evenly balanced blends of all three styles, distracting salespeople from discovering needs and wants as they waste their time and energy hopelessly focusing on marginally significant insights. It can be fascinating to watch as they bend themselves into pretzels trying to figure out into which category a prospect fits.

Whenever I encounter someone I think has been trained in recognizing learning styles, I like to have a little fun by saying things such as, "I don't see it that way because what I'm hearing just doesn't feel right."

This is a popular technique, sold as a relatively easy way to create a comfortable connection with prospects. However, it's anything but easy because the science is flawed. Ani Aharonian writes at skeptic.com, "Perhaps this idea has taken strong hold because it is an appealing one. It is consistent with our desire to perceive ourselves as individuals, it is a positive and optimistic proposition that each person has equivalent potential to learn if the instruction can be matched to their individual learning style."

Look, this is a large, diverse field of study that experts disagree on, not a simplistic sales technique you can learn in an hour-long class. So rather than spending time working on these types of arcane concepts, put your energy into the one technique that always pays off: honesty.

If you want your prospect to trust you, then you must trust yourself first, and that's not going to happen if your entire repertoire is built around devious practices. Be honest and open and give her a chance to get to know you, instead of employing hackneyed methods for wrestling control of the interview and forcing your agenda.

Be respectful and considerate, and show a genuine interest in her. Deal with what is important to her, not what's important to you. And above all, be yourself because nobody can do that better than you, or as life coach extraordinaire Dr. Seuss put it, "Today you are You, that is truer than true. There is no one alive who is Youer than You."

26

Of Profiles, Roles and Pigeonholes, Part 4

Do you remember July 12, 1979, when Chicago radio shock jock Steve Dahl killed disco? If you were too young or not yet born, then you missed one of the most curious conclusions to a period of much maligned musical history. Dahl facilitated a disco record bombing at Comiskey Park during a baseball doubleheader between the White Sox and the Tigers, a pyrotechnic stunt that went sideways quickly and damaged the infield so severely that Chicago had to forfeit the second game. *Le Freak* Dahl created such a *Night Fever* with his *Disco Inferno* because of his inexplicably intense hatred for a genre of dance music that was fun and harmless. And I was like, "Yo, Steve: *Don't Leave Me this Way*, man; *You Should Be Dancing* instead of burning discs, but instead, you orchestrated the *Last Dance*, leaving me and my brethren-Tony Maneros with closets full of three-piece, pastel suits; colorfully patterned, huge-collared shirts; gold chains galore; and glitter platform shoes. Nice try, but *I'm Stayin' Alive*, dude, and *I Will Survive* as I Hustle, Bump, Funky Chicken and Robot onward and upward."

Well, maybe my chicken's not as funky as it once was and I may bump (into things) a bit more than I hustle these days, although my robot is becoming authentic as they continue to replace body parts with mechanical doohickeys. However, I'm still groovin' on disco, or should I say discs — DISC profiles that is — and although I may be groovin', I'm not altogether approvin', and sometimes even disapprovin'.

Now please, take a beat before you go all ape feces on me and get out the pitchforks and torches — let me 'splain.

But first some context: DISC is a behavioral assessment tool based on the theories of psychologist William Marston (inventor of the lie detector and creator of Wonder Woman), which centers on four different behavioral traits, and supposedly allows people to recognize dominant human characteristics. The program is not simply about understanding oneself better, but also about understanding others.

Through a series of questions, DISC assessment catalogs people into four categories: **Dominance** (a person who places emphasis on accomplishing results, the bottom line, confidence); **Influence** (a person who places emphasis on influencing or persuading others, openness, relationships); **Steadiness** (a person who places emphasis on cooperation, sincerity, dependability); and **Conscientiousness** (a person who places emphasis on quality and accuracy, expertise, competency).

Typical questions on the assessment go something like:

The way I see myself most, is ...
    1. Doing, driving and accomplishing.
    2. Patient, kind and helpful.
    3. Logical, factual and correct.
    4. Friendly, fun and persuasive.

When working on a team and we encounter a difficulty of some kind, I am most likely to say ...
    1. Lighten up! Just go with the flow.
    2. Let's make a decision.
    3. How do you feel? I'd like to make sure that everyone is comfortable.
    4. Let's consider this more carefully. Do we have all the data we need?

When someone on my team offers a solution to a problem and I disagree, I ...
1. Laugh out loud until coffee runs out of my nose.
2. Throw what's left of my coffee at them.
3. Point out how totally stupid they are.
4. Let the air out of their car tires.

Would you give any credence to a test based on theories postulated by the guy who created Wonder Woman?
1. Are you kidding? Have you seen her outfit?
2. The character was based on Olive Byrne, Marston and his wife's life partner ... WTF?
3. A couple's life partner ... WTF?
4. WTF?

Proponents of the popular assessments advocate these benefits:
- ➢ Increase self-knowledge of how you respond to conflict, what motivates you, what causes you stress and how you solve problems.
- ➢ Acquire an understanding of other people's strengths and weaknesses.
- ➢ Learn how to adapt your style to get along better with others.
- ➢ Foster constructive and creative group interactions.
- ➢ Facilitate better teamwork and minimize team conflict.
- ➢ Develop stronger sales skills by identifying and responding to customer styles.
- ➢ Manage more effectively by understanding the dispositions and priorities of employees and team members.
- ➢ Become more of a well-rounded and effective leader.
- ➢ Discover why so many people think you're not so pimpalicious.

You can unearth tons of material off the internet on DISC assessment, some of it informative, some instructive, some snake-oil hype and some realistic evaluations and informed practical usage. In a piece from ttisi.com, I found a short but fairly accurate assessment of the assessment: "DISC has enjoyed immense popularity and acceptance in HR and among consultants since the late 1980s. With its broad, long-established and passionate fan base, we sometimes find consultants, coaches and trainers can have a tendency to see people dynamics through the lens of this single tool. Sometimes, this means DISC is used to explain things about people beyond the scope of what it is actually designed to measure, while ignoring other important elements of human personality."

And that's my biggest problem with the DISC assessment: It tends to be used like it's the holy grail of workplace dynamics when it's not anything close to that — it's merely a tool to help gain insight into human interaction, if that's a problem for your group. In working with sales teams, I find it's not always the case.

I once put that theory to a test. I would use DISC assessment during the fourth session of my sales classes, and one time before I administered the assessment, I wrote a list of the four categories and their characteristics on the board. I then had my students list everybody else's name and decide if their classmates' strongest personality traits fell into D, I, S or C. Guess what? They were a fairy's breath away from 100 percent accurate. That's because they had gotten to know each other over the preceding three sessions, and, like in all human contact, they developed a conscious or subconscious understanding of each other's strengths and weaknesses, and they were able to identify those features rather easily.

Duh!

Really, human understanding is intuitive; it was part of the package that came along with the snake and the apple. All you have to do to use that gift is listen and observe, and forget your own precious agenda for a moment while concentrating on somebody else.

For a change?

Maybe?

It sounds simple, I know, but in practice, it's difficult to do. Which is why a profile test can help, especially if your group is self-conscious and reticent. A good trainer, using these evaluation results, can assist people in obtaining a better understanding of each other and promote a more productive system of communications, but she can't make a silk purse out of the galactically obtuse.

The other problem I have is that nobody is defined by a single DISC style. Actually, your style is a blend of these four primary personality types and other lesser-known types. And making it even more difficult to pigeonhole, a person's personality can oscillate. You can be a high D one day and a high I the next, depending on your mood and circumstances. It's all very subjective and not really as scientific as we're led to believe. In reality, a DISC assessment is a device that can help recognize some heretofore unknown obstacles and assist in starting a positive and constructive conversation.

But don't take it too seriously, like I don't. Honestly, I'm not sure the assessment ever gets it right. I've taken the test several times and it keeps coming up with the same disturbing results — it says I'm a high D I C.

27

Of Profiles, Roles and Pigeonholes, Conclusion

You think I'm a whore, but I got a heart of gold.
You're lockin' your doors; you're leavin' me out in the cold.

Martin Freeman, aka Bilbo Baggins, said, "Any pigeonhole is something to be rebelled against." That's an understandable sentiment for an actor who played a memorable middle earthling to international fame in *The Hobbit* trilogy, and in so doing, created a character with whom he would come to be closely identified. Just ask Leonard Nimoy (perhaps a séance?) how hard it is to climb out of a stereotype once you show up in big ears. But exceptional pinna isn't the only thing that can get you stuck in a pigeonhole, fighting like a desperate salmon against the raging forces of a swift and enveloping current of entrenched, albeit misguided perception.

Like me, the desperate salmon.

I've been pigeonholed my entire life, so you could say I'm a bit of an expert on the subject. And like my doppelganger, Jim Rockford, I can be a bit sensitive about it, too. In "The Dexter Crisis" episode, when Charles Dexter (played by Tim O'Connor) reacts negatively to Rockford's rate of $200 a day plus expenses (like almost every other potential client in the show's six-year run), Rockford gives him some what-for.

"You're a little touchy there," Dexter observes.

"Right, I'm a little touchy," Rockford responds, crabbily.

And that's exactly how I feel about pigeonholing: crabby —

a crabby, desperate salmon; a simmering seafood, blue-plate special!

It all started when I was a young boy at Riverton Public School. It was a public school, but could have just as well been a Christian school. That's because everybody in the place was a good Christian, most notably the ones who weren't allowed to play with me. They weren't allowed to play with me because I was being raised by a single, divorced mother, relatively unheard of and certainly unwelcomed in Riverton, New Jersey, in the 1950s. As I recall, there were only three kids in school whose parents were divorced: me, my sister and a boy named Fred. Besides having mothers who wore a scarlet letter, and other than being summarily ostracized, the only thing Fred and I had in common was that we lived in apartments, another objectionable pigeonhole to be avoided in the tree-lined streets of pietistic sanctimony of my bewildering youth.

So, somewhere along the line, I turned that judgmental repudiation inward and became a rather obnoxious and unmotivated kid, to the point where they called my mother into school for a conference. They wanted to talk about my behavior and my aptitude.

Like, what's up?

The gist of the conversation was that I should be thinking about a career in the trades, perhaps a carpenter or plumber. Apparently, they didn't appreciate my creative genius lying just beneath the surface of my youthful effervescence, and thought a job working with my hands instead of my brain would be most appropriate (as if carpenters and plumbers were scarecrows who had no brains). What they didn't know was that my mother had a brother who was a carpenter and a brother who was plumber, so the meeting didn't go too well. And ironically, up until that moment, I wanted to be a carpenter, but instead, I went to college where I used my brain to think and my hands to write and graduated in two-and-a-half years with high honors.

Assigning roles and pigeonholing can be a dangerous

undertaking, and if you're not careful, they can sometimes *throw that speedball by you, make you look like a fool, boy.*

Another result of that momentous meeting was that I began to develop a persona that would, for the rest of my life, define me in the eyes of pigeonholers galore: I started to affect a veneer of confidence and detachment that people to this day assume comes from a life of privilege, like I'm a snob.

Ha! I grew up on hand-me-down clothes and TV dinners. I thought refinement was an occasional meal of goldenrod eggs. We shopped at secondhand stores, and I guess I looked it because in the seventh grade, after discovering sports and using them to claw my way up the ladder of social strata, I was finally invited to a cool kids party. And as the ironies piled on, one of the cool boys took me aside and asked me what I was going to wear. He told me not to dress like I normally did; to find something more presentable. Wow! And guess what? That was one of the kids who wasn't allowed to play with me growing up. His mother was a big mahoff at the Methodist church, and she didn't go for divorce or any of its entanglements.

Like me — entanglement extraordinaire.

So I went to that party dressed in new clothes (that I bought with money from my paper route), and ended up dating the coolest girl in school, a girl who had, up until that party, been the girlfriend of the schmuck who told me to dress appropriately.

Ironies overfloweth!

Like my first semester in college. I was in a 200-level course that I wasn't eligible for, and I think it was a source of intrigue and irritation for the ponytailed professor — she had a disquieting way of looking at me, like I was being examined under glass. The class was Modern Drama, and I had picked it simply because it fit my schedule perfectly, and because it was forbidden.

Rebellious arrogance dies hard.

In order to take a 200-level course, you needed English Lit

101 and a world literature survey course, but since it was my first semester, I had completed neither. I don't remember the exact details, but using my yet-to-be acknowledged sales skills, I talked my way past my advisor and the folks at registration and into the firm grip of Dr. Strangelove, who can still send shivers down my back thinking of her.

Toward the end of the semester, we were divided into groups of four to complete a project on an assigned play. Ours was *A Dream Play* by August Strindberg, an extremely inscrutable and peculiar piece. We were to make an oral presentation to the class on four different aspects of the play — history of the play, about the playwright, a synopsis and a critique — and we would receive individual grades based on our performance combined with the performance of the group. I drew the synopsis, the least sexy task and the most perfunctory.

Everybody else on my team got an A; I got a C. I immediately went to Dr. Ponytailed Strangelove to ask why.

"To be perfectly honest," she said through an enigmatic smile, "your synopsis was kind of boring."

Did she just wink at me?

"Synopses, by definition, are boring," I responded. "I worked very hard on it, and as you know, the play is really difficult to penetrate. I think I had the hardest synopsis in the class, and you gave everybody else in my group an A."

"Yes, I did. Do you wonder why?"

I'm sure she winked this time.

"Of course I wonder why. That's why I'm here," I almost seethed.

"Well," she started, "you don't belong in this class. It was a mistake jumping you up, and I was against it from the beginning. But mainly it's because I think you've gotten by far too long on the strength of your trusting looks and winning charm. I believe that's why you're even here."

Is this woman nuts? What's she talking about? I'm being judged and graded on some intangible and arbitrary definition of who I am? I'm being pigeonholed as a smooth-talking lightweight? I didn't know what to say. I could only sit there staring at her.

Finally, I asked, incredulously, "So you don't like my attitude and that's why I got a C?"

"No," she replied. "I find your attitude extremely attractive, but I gave you the C for your own good."

Once again, I was speechless. For a moment. "So, you gave me a C because you like my bad attitude?"

She laughed and grabbed the grade card from my hand. She crossed out the C and replaced it with a B. "I'm changing your grade," she said, "because of your delightful wit."

Gee? I wondered. What would I have to do to get an A? Let her jump my bones, or whatever the hell was going on there?

Then I got into sales and the profiling began in earnest. The day I donned my first suit and picked up a sales bag, I was pigeonholed for the rest of my life: A salesman! *Pack up the babies and grab the old ladies* and hide your daughters — salesman in town! It's been a lifelong battle to overcome that negative perception, but, unfortunately, most of it is well-earned. I've written extensively about the predicament *we few, we happy few, we band of brothers* (and sisters, to update Shakespeare a bit) find ourselves in daily as we battle the dragons of self-imposed boundaries and blockades.

Well, I have some news for the sacred brotherhood of drummers, canvassers and knockers: It ain't gettin' better any time soon. And that's good news because if it did get better, if it got easier to sell, then anyone could do it. The built-in resistance of being pigeonholed as a slick hustler is hard to deal with, for sure, but the rewards can be great if you can persevere and conquer those myriad dragons, but not as hard to surmount as some other pigeonholes.

Like a pigeonhole one of my sons was profiled into early in his young life. He was diagnosed with ADHD and dyslexia and spent the rest of his scholastic career trying to overcome not just the afflictions, but the associated stereotype.

"ADHD stands for attention deficit hyperactivity disorder, a condition with symptoms such as inattentiveness, impulsivity, and hyperactivity," according to webmd.com. "The symptoms differ from person to person. ADHD was formerly called ADD, or attention deficit disorder. Both children and adults can have ADHD, but the symptoms always begin in childhood. Adults with ADHD may have trouble managing time, being organized, setting goals, and holding down a job." The Centers for Disease Control and Prevention says that 11 percent of American children, ages 7 to 14 have an attention disorder, but if you go to any public school today, you'll see a lot more than 11 percent of the boys lining up in the morning for their Ritalin. That's because boys are three times more likely to be diagnosed with ADHD than their female peers, and girls are diagnosed on average five years later than boys, and because the condition is grossly underreported or undiagnosed.

ADHD is not really a disease, per se, but rather a condition characterized by a set of associated symptoms that is treated with amphetamine or methylphenidate medications, most notably Adderall, Concerta, Vyvanse, Strattera and the aforementioned and popular Ritalin. Many famous people have ADHD, such as Michael Jordan, Justin Timberlake, Michael Phelps, Howie Mandel, Adam Levine, Paris Hilton and The Fonz. And some brilliant ones too, such as Bill Gates, Albert Einstein and Leonardo da Vinci.

That collection of overachievers did little to help my son, however, because once diagnosed, he was put into special education, or Speds, as they were derisively called by his follow students of high moral dissimulation. (Where's Holden Caulfield when you need him?) It was a designation of the lowest order, maybe the worst sort of slur available to the socially conscious deriders of everything unclick-worthy. And Speds were definitely unclick-worthy, not just to the other students, but to the faculty as well who, generally, considered them stupid and destined for jobs like carpenter and plumber.

Profiling and pigeonholing are hard to eradicate in a system built on deportment and the singularly unremarkable ability to memorize, a system designed to promote the development of the masses but not necessarily capable of nurturing the different, other than to babysit and move along. Well, they moved my son along all right; not by their choice, by his. He not only went to college and graduated with a degree in business management, but he had to take Statistics. Do you hear that, all you scholastic pigeonholers? He had to take and pass Stats, considered one of the hardest courses in college.

And he's not too bad with a hammer and plunger, either.

Walter Isaacson has a prodigious biography out about Leonardo da Vinci, wherein he speculates that if The Master were alive today, he would be diagnosed with ADHD at an early age and drugged all through his school years, thereby negating or obscuring his brilliance and damaging one of the most extraordinary minds of all time. It's an interesting thought and makes you wonder how many Einsteins and da Vincis we're suppressing today under the pretense of inclusion that is, in reality, a movement to homogenize society.

It's my belief that we have it all ass-backwards. I believe a much larger percentage of the population has ADHD than commonly known, maybe even more than half, which would make it the norm. Perhaps we should start treating those who tend to sit still and focus with some kind of wonder drug to get them up and fidgeting. Maybe all our structures of rules and curriculums have been designed by a corps of constipated lackies limited to attention and restraint. Maybe everything we know is wrong and holding us back, and it's time to let the Speds loose to fix things up.

Maybe.

And maybe it's already happening. (After all, Bill Gates is one of us.) You see that thing at the end of your arm, the rectangled object that's practically attached to your hand, the one buzzing and chirping and flashing? You think it's a phone, I know, but it's really a Scramblyzer. Watch everyone around you — you see it all the time, everywhere you go: A person will be sitting there calm and chilling and focusing on something and quick as *Jumpin' Jack Flash*, the arm shoots up accompanied by rapid thumb movement and unfocus is instantly restored.

Voilà!

It's a beautiful thing for the institutionally marginalized.

And pigeonholed!

As I mentioned, my son had the added burden of dyslexia, a learning disorder that affects the ability to read, spell, write and speak. People who suffer from dyslexia often are intelligent and hardworking, but they have trouble connecting the letters. About 5 to 10 percent of Americans have some symptoms of dyslexia, including Steven Spielberg, Magic Johnson, Tom Cruise and The Fonz (a two-time winner!). Albert Einstein (also a two-time winner), Pablo Picasso and Mohammad Ali also suffered from the affliction.

Like The Fonz, Albert Einstein and my son, it's not unusual for someone to suffer from both ADHD and dyslexia, as another famous person did whom you'd never guess: President John Fitzgerald Kennedy. Like almost everything else about JFK, that little gem is fervently protected by the Kennedy Clan, hellbent on keeping the pretense of Camelot alive. Another one of those secrets was the president's bad back. He first hurt it while in high school when his chauffeur playfully tackled him, and further aggravated it during World War II when his PT boat was rammed and sunk. As a result, JFK suffered serious back pain the rest of this life. To combat it, he took painkillers and wore a back brace, and it was that back brace that directly led to his demise.

When the first bullet hit him from behind, it should have knocked him over on his side and into Jackie's lap. Unfortunately for the world, that brace propped him up and rendered him a sitting duck for the fatal shot from the front that blew away a large part of his scalp and brain. Perhaps if his bad back had been public knowledge, maybe something could have been done to allow him more freedom of movement, but he was packaged and sold as the embodiment of youth and vigor, and any sign of infirmity, he believed, would have pigeonholed him as weak. It's ironic that his famous book, *Profiles in Courage,* was something that ultimately couldn't be said about him because he didn't have the courage to expose his own debility; to risk being unfairly profiled.

Much like another president, Franklin Delano Roosevelt, who was crippled by polio and tried to hide if from the world for the same reasons Kennedy did: He didn't want to be profiled and pigeonholed as a sick and frail man. Both of these men wanted to be seen as strong and forceful, and they feared being stereotyped. That's too bad — think how many sufferers of polio might have been helped or encouraged if FDR had been more honest and open about his disease. A great opportunity lost, and, in my opinion, he would have been remembered as a much stronger man and leader.

We're all subject to profiles, roles and pigeonholes, and, apparently, getting older doesn't abate the situation any. I mean, sometimes it feels like I'm being s*et up, like a bowlin' pin. Knocked down, it gets to wearin' thin. They just won't let you be.*

Not too long ago, we were out to dinner and as I was leaving the restaurant, a group of young people were entering. I held the door for them, and as the last fellow in line passed me, he said, "Thank you, sir."

What?!

And that seemed to start an avalanche. Everywhere I went, people were all, "Good morning, sir. How're you doing, sir? Nice to see you, sir."

Sir!!!

Look, I know it's a term of respect and endearment, but it's for old people, not me! I'm not a sir, *nobody calls me sir. You got the wrong guy. I'm the dude, man.* That's right, *I'm the Dude, so that's what you call me. That or, His Dudeness, or Duder, or El Duderino, if you're not into the whole brevity thing.* So, let's dispense with the "sir" stuff until I reach a point of dudeless-dotage. In the meantime, next time you see me, maybe a quick fist pump and a simple "Duuuuuuuuuuude!"

This pigeon has flown the coop.

28

and speaking of getting old ...

According to Mark Twain, age is an issue of mind over matter. If you don't mind, it doesn't matter. George Burns was once asked, who wants to be 95? His response: a 94-year-old. Groucho Marx once said that anyone can get old; all you have to do is live long enough. And Red Skelton added that there are three ages of man: youth, middle age and "you're looking well."

Ha, ha, right?

Everybody jokes about getting old because, let's face it, it's funny, hilarious, a real bone tickler, until, of course, it happens to you. Then, not so much. Especially if you're trying to get a loan, a mortgage, health insurance, life insurance or a date online (where lying about age is practically a requirement, along with lying about your weight). Even more disgruntling, if you're looking for a job after you've crossed the Mendoza Line of birthdays, then the joke's on you, or to paraphrase Bluto's discerning line from *Animal House*: "You screwed up; you lived too long."

Don't think it's a major problem? My guess is you're under 50. But don't worry, it'll come to you (if you're lucky). Other than funeral homes, few businesses are interested in us older folk. We're just not in with the in-crowd any longer, and if you don't believe that, try finding gainful employment if you're old enough to join AARP. Sad truth be told, the older you get, the harder it gets ...

... to find a job, that is. End of discussion. Thanks for the memories and don't let the door hit you in the ass. Unfortunately for all us original Mouseketeers as we tack on the years, job hunting becomes exponentially more difficult.

According to Melissa Evans at citylab.com, "The Age Discrimination in Employment Act of 1967 prohibits employment discrimination based on age for people 40 and older. But that hasn't stopped it from becoming pervasive. Nearly two-thirds of workers aged 45 to 74 say they have experienced age discrimination in the workplace, according to a study by AARP, and 92 percent of those who did, said it was common. And bad news, millennials: One expert believes it can kick in as young as 35."

She added that studies have found that "younger job applicants are much more likely to get a callback than people in their mid-60s with similar experience, and that discrimination against older women, particularly, is rampant. Employers value older workers' knowledge, but may view them as less flexible, less willing to learn new things, and expensive, compared to younger candidates."

Sure, I understand. I'm less flexible in some areas of my life, but I make up for any deficiency in limberness with attitude and stick-to-itiveness. Yet, when it comes to learning new things or trying different approaches, I can bend with the best of them. Getting older does not necessarily equate to obstinance and rigidity. On the contrary, look at Stephen King, in his 70s and still scaring the bejesus out of people; Nancy Pelosi, in her late 70s and still scaring the bejesus out of people; Keith Richards, indeterminate age and still scaring the bejesus out of people.

Age discrimination really is a sad state of affairs, but self-styled positivity guru Emile Ratelband is going to fix all of that. He believes age is just a number, and his is a number this Dutchman wants to change. Mike Corder of the Associated Press writes, "The 69-year-old TV personality has asked a court in the Netherlands to approve his request for a new birthday that officially would make him 49." Ratelband wants to shift his birthday from March 11, 1949, to March 11, 1969, comparing the change to identifying as transgender. He says his legal appeal is consistent with other forms of personal transformation that are gaining acceptance and government recognition in the Netherlands and around the world.

Right on, brother! No longer will we be tied down by the man's oppressive shackles of judgmental agedness; no longer will we be discarded on the dung heap of senescence, dotage and feebleness; no longer will we stand for being prejudicially labeled infirm and senile simply because we forget what day it is or why we came into the kitchen; no longer will we ... wait, I forgot where I was going here.

Anyway, consider this wise old chestnut: "How old would you be if you didn't know how old you are?" That and a cup of coffee won't help you get a mortgage, but it sounds really cool. Unfortunately, the only cure for getting old is death, *and dying to me don't sound like all that much fun.* So, I'll continue to put one foot in front of the other and pick my fights, like my latest crusade: In my exhaustive research into the inequities of life, it has come to my attention that a local nudist camp is offering a discount to people under 40. Apparently, they're trying to spruce up the joint and uplift the overall condition of its exposees, and other than the indigenous and bucolic weeping willows, all things droopy are unencouraged to show their goods.

I'm offended!

I identify as a 35-year-old and I believe it is my right to be treated as the age I'm hardwired to be, not some arbitrary number affixed to the monotonous rotations of the sun. I'm so enraged that I'm starting a movement to picket the camp with the slogan, "If there ain't no wrinkles, then there ain't no tingles."

As soon as I take a nap.

29

The Dog Kicker, et al.

If you're trying to sell somebody something, it's probably not a good idea to kick his dog.

Do you think?

But that's what happened to me several years ago when I was buying a copy machine, before copy machines were part of the fabulous information age, packaged as digital-do-it-alls: copiers, printers, faxes, scanners, pencil sharpeners, foot massagers, etc.

I had shopped around and conducted as much research as I could, given the limited resources at my disposal during the Paleolithic Age of technology, before *the beauty, the splendor, the wonder of* Google. And I had made up my mind what I wanted: a state-of-the-art marvel that could run 25 black and white copies per minute, with zoom capabilities and two built-in trays that held different-sized paper.

Whoop-de-do!

You had to lease those monsters back then because they were way too expensive for a small business to buy, forcing you to do business with a dealer — the then-current incarnation of used-car salesmen. It was a competitive field and those guys were ruthless with their high-pressure approach, so kicking a dog here or there along the way was not completely out of character.

I didn't like the guy right off, but he worked for the only dealer in town with the brand I wanted, and I pulled the lucky straw when I walked into the store. He was a real meathead, blond hair, stupid smile and muscled (before it was cool to be muscled, when only real meatheads lifted weights). He was pushy, obnoxious and completely disinterested in my needs or wants.

I bought the machine anyway.

When he delivered it, my big, friendly golden retriever met him at the door, tail wagging and happy as all get-out to see him. Meathead was busy carrying in the machine and didn't have time for all creatures great or small, so he kicked my dog out of the way.

I was shocked — the guy just kicked my dog!

A rather heated conversation ensued where he first denied it, then said the dog jumped on him. Unfortunately, I had to deal with that firm for service over the next three years of the lease, but since then I've started and operated several businesses and spent hundreds of thousands of dollars on office equipment, and I never spent another dime with that Neanderthal's company.

Not to mention my negative reviews to anybody who would listen.

Such is the power of an ineffective salesperson: They will cost you much more in bad-will than the positive results an effective salesperson can produce. In fact, according to the White House Office of Consumer Affairs, a dissatisfied customer will tell between nine and 15 people about his experience. Around 13 percent of dissatisfied customers tell more than 20 people.

That's a lot of bad publicity from one meathead, so as a public service, the following is a list of some scurrilous-fermenting fellows and fellowettes to avoid:

1. <u>The Dog Kicker:</u> This is Meathead, as previously described. He (or she — and yes ladies, you too can be meatheads) is aggressive, forceful, loud-mouthed, insensitive and, in general, repulsive. You can spot him by his Palm Springs tan, dripping gold jewelry, monosyllabic vocabulary and ankle socks.

2. <u>The Monty Hall:</u> Monty Hall was the long-time host of *Let's Make a Deal,* a TV game show where people dressed up in outlandish costumes in hopes of getting noticed by Monty and picked to bid on fabulous prizes or worthless gags behind Door No. 1, Door No. 2, or Door No. 3. This type of salesperson is always trying to make a deal rather than sell you on her product's merits. When a prospect tells her he has no interest, her natural response is to offer to cut price. That's like telling the dentist your teeth don't hurt and him saying, "In that case, I'll only pull out a couple." Beware of choosing the wrong door with this one because the gag is almost always on you.

3. <u>The Solicitor Whisperer:</u> These are the folks who speak so softly, you need to strain to pick out a word here and there just to follow their drift. Mumblers and high-pitched-squeakers also fall into this category. They are so hard to hear, you eventually stop listening and simply smile and nod your head, but that, like in an episode of *Seinfeld,* can lead to disaster. In Jerry's case, he ended up agreeing to wear a puffy shirt that made him look like a deranged pirate during an appearance on *The Tonight Show.* My advice is to make them put everything in writing, or you may find yourself walking the plank, matey. Arrrrrr!

4. <u>Slippery Sid & Shady Sadie:</u> These are the "Tell you what I'm gonna do" back-slappers and arm-squeezers who make you feel like you need a shower after a brief encounter. They always wear a smarmy smile and dot their speech with a serpentine tongue, as their eyes dart back and forth in a hypnotic, satanic ritual of, "You can trust me." Don't! To protect yourself, keep a wooden stake and silver bullet with you at all times.

5. <u>The Stephen King:</u> These folks try to frighten the hell out of you with dire predictions of certain catastrophe if you don't buy their service or product, like the insurance salesman who tells you, "I guarantee you're going to die. I also guarantee that this insurance policy will protect you." Against what? Other predator insurance salesmen trying to scare the bejesus out of me with their *Dead Zone* repartee; a guy who says he'll *Stand*

by *Me* but ends up a real *Misery*; who comes on like *The Shining*, but I end up *Walking the Green Mile* alone; who I believe is *It*, but quickly learn he's from *The Dark Tower*? No thank you — this *Bag of Bones* hasn't reached that level of *Desperation*.

6. <u>The Rapper:</u> He's the know-it-all who talks, talks, talks, not allowing you to get a word in edgewise. Not to be confused with <u>Nervous Nell</u>, the nervous talker. Just as nature abhors a vacuum, some salespeople abhor silence, and when the conversation lags, they start baying like a hyena. I've used this line before, but it's so true that it bears repeating, and repeating, and repeating: It is written that Samson slew thousands of Philistines with the jawbone of an ass, and it is said that thousands of sales are killed every day using the same weapon. Accordingly, my advice to salespeople everywhere: Shut up!

And try not to kick the prospect's dog.

Do you think?

30

Adjustment Bureau

Back in the dark ages of child-rearing, I played youth baseball. I started when I was 6 years old, but we didn't have tee-ball or dad-pitch or face masks or even batting helmets; we didn't have Gatorade or batting gloves or personal bat bags, and none of those soft, rubberized baseballs; we didn't have scoreboards or outfield fences or dugouts and no refreshment stands or fundraisers.

We didn't even get participation trophies.

We just had fun.

That was before parents felt the compulsion to be there for all the minutiae of our prepubescent, preferably pedantic, precisely pedestrian lives.

In those days we weren't commodities. We were just kids.

That was the first year my town had organized teams for kids under high-school age, and the level I played at was called Midgets. Midgets was for kids from ages 7 to 9, and since I was 6, I wasn't eligible. However, even back then I had a hard time taking no for an answer, so I hung around the fields and tried to talk my way onto a team.

I wasn't having much luck until one day a team was trying to recruit a player to be the catcher, but there were no takers. Being the salesman I was to be, I saw an opportunity and volunteered, and *voilà*, I was a Midget.

Now, at that time, I probably didn't even know what a catcher was, but I strapped on the bulky, cumbersome equipment and dragged my undersized body laden with oversized accoutrement behind the plate and allowed boys three years older to throw hard and fast baseballs at me with evil intent.

And let me tell you, those pitches could really sting. I didn't care much for the stinging, so eventually I figured out that if the ball was coming in too fast, I'd let it go and it would pop off the umpire's chest protector or facemask. After a while, the umps stopped crouching behind me and went out and stood behind the pitcher.

We all learn to make adjustments.

Or we don't.

I met with a business owner recently who fell into the "don't" category, and his company was suffering because of it. It seems perfectly reasonable to assume that all businesses must make periodic adjustments relative to the conditions of the market, the competition and, most importantly, their own internal dynamics, but you know how it is when we make assumptions.

Fortunately for guys like me, who earn their daily bread consulting with companies gone wild, that assumption would be seriously spurious.

This particular fellow had been in business for many years and was successful for most of that time, but since the great post-Glass-Steagall-Act run of insatiably avaricious Wall Street money-grabbers tumbled the economy into the Houdiniesque, manually dexterous hands of our best and brightest political manipulators, sales nosedived and the once robust and reliable revenue stream dwindled down to a drip barely adequate enough to float the ship.

The operation had been leaking for years and was trapped in a seemingly inexorable death spiral, slowly descending to the bottom of the cold, dark sea.

We talked for a while about what sales efforts had been like in the past and what they were today, and they really weren't very different at all. As a matter of fact, the business owner staunchly defended the approach he had used for years to build his organization, an approach that had produced tremendous profits.

When I asked what he planned to do to fix the problems, he said they were going to have to focus more and work harder.

"In other words," I asked, "you're going to take the things you're doing now that aren't working and do more of them?"

He stared at me for a moment with a crooked smile and finally said, "Well, when you put it like that, it sounds pretty stupid. I guess I need to rethink this."

Changes in latitudes, changes in attitudes, nothing remains quite the same.

It should be obvious that every business needs to make adjustments to stay viable and competitive, but sometimes it's hard to see that necessity or the possible solutions from inside the box. Making adjustments should be a part of every business' DNA, and those adjustments should not be a leap of faith: they should be a well-thought-out, diligently executed plan. And they don't have to be draconian resections — that's where a good outside consultant comes into play. As Jenny Rogers writes in *Manager as Coach: The New Way to Get Results*, "Through coaching, people are able to find their own solutions, develop their own skills, and change their own attitudes and behaviors." As convoluted as it may sound, a more insightful perspective can best be achieved through others' perspectives.

Like how I was able to make necessary changes as a result of the umpires' disgruntled perspectives. Once they were no longer there as my backstop, I had to learn to catch the ball, and, as a result, I eventually became a pretty good catcher. But that only lasted until I discovered girls. That's when I moved to third base. At third base, I didn't get as sweaty or dirty, had more opportunities to make hero plays, and could spy the PYTs in the stands from a better vantage point.

We all learn to make adjustments.

31

Unsocial Media

'Twas brillig, and the slithy toves
Did gyre and gimble in the wabe:
All mimsy were the borogoves,
And the mome raths outgrabe.

Got it?

That's the opening stanza from the poem *Jabberwocky*, written by Lewis Carroll in 1871, and included in *Through the Looking Glass*, the sequel to *Alice's Adventures in Wonderland*. At first blush, it doesn't make much sense, and, indeed, is usually described as a nonsense poem. However, while in college, I wrote a paper on its meaning, and I was rather astonished at how much scholarly study existed on the subject. Of course, that was in the time before Google, so, in order to unearth those references, I had to spend many hours in the library (where I usually went only to catch a quick nap or hit on unsuspecting coeds with my cleverly disguised intellectual approach). Today, thanks to the ubiquitous and insidiously insinuating internet, I could do the same amount of work in about 20 minutes.

Such is the marvel of modern binary-coded magic.

The world is now at our fingertips, but, truth be told, we don't have a clue what to do with it. For the vast majority of us ex-knuckle-dragging troglodytes, most of it makes about as much sense as *Jabberwocky*, especially when it comes to the latest-with-the-greatest, hyper-overhyped media sensation: social media.

You can't listen to a business broadcast or open a business publication or go to a business event or climb the highest mountain to get away from it all without hearing about the promotional power of omnipotent social media. The ubiquitous pounding of the social media drum beats loud and clear from every neophyte internet marketing maven, like Indians on a ridge surrounding the wagon train in the old Western movies, blathering on and on about the unbelievable potential of sharing your business identity with the other indispensable information of our times, like Aunt Ethel wishing you a glorious day of peace and solitude (like you'll ever find any of that on a social media site).

So, the question is, can social media help brand your business?

Sure, if done correctly with relevant content and proper timing. Otherwise, it can make you look like a frivolous fool with way too much time on your hands.

Which is what social media does best.

Like Pavlov's dog, we're being taught to salivate at the sight or sound of certain stimuli, incessantly dripping on our consciousness; a Chinese water torture of B.F. Skinner's applied principle of reinforcement. Day after day, taking over our rational gray matter and replacing it with simplistic and inane banality.

Drip, drip, drip.

As the band plays on.

Drip, drip, drip.

As it becomes curiouser and curiouser.

Drip, drip, drip.

As we get stupider and stupider.

Don't believe it?

According to the Statistic Brain Research Institute website, in 2015, the average person had an attention span of 8.25 seconds. (The average goldfish's attention span is nine seconds.) The average back in 2000 was 12 seconds.

Scary? Yet every day, every hour, every minute, we're pulling off the information highway at rest stops called Facebook or Twitter or Instagram, all with large multicolored, blinking neon lights that read "Abandon all hope, ye who enter here."

And as we frolic *in the autumn mist in a land called Honah Lee*, we begin to sound a bit like Alice in her conversation with the Cheshire Cat:

"But I don't want to go among mad people," Alice remarked.

"Oh, you can't help that," said the Cat: "We're all mad here. I'm mad. You're mad."

"How do you know I'm mad?" said Alice.

"You must be," said the Cat, "or you wouldn't have come here."

Yes, we're all mad, and getting madder all the time. I'm sure you've seen this very applicable-to-the-subject-at-hand quote countless times at your favorite rest stop: "The difference between stupidity and genius is that genius has its limits." That quote is credited to Albert Einstein, but the problem is, he never said it (according to *The Ultimate Quotable Einstein* from Princeton University Press). However, truth and facts will never stop the juggernaut of social media once it gets rolling downhill, taking us with it, unstoppable, leaving a vacuous trail of nattering nincompoops grinning like the Cheshire Cat.

The real Einstein quote that this cute and superficial aphorism is believed to have derived from is, "The majority of the stupid is invincible and guaranteed for all time. The terror of their tyranny, however, is alleviated by their lack of consistency." If you're having trouble understanding this elevated language, ask a goldfish for help.

Social media and stupidity are not necessarily interchangeable concepts, but they're close cousins, and if you're not careful, you will be pulled down into the muck and mire. Mark Twain said it best 150 years before folly traveled at the speed of light: "Never argue with stupid people, they will drag you down to their level and then beat you with experience."

When it comes to using social media to promote your business, keep in mind that it can be a valuable tool or a colossal nightmare, depending on whether you're astute enough to recognize it for what it is. It has its benefits, its limits and its danger, and the danger often comes disguised as a benefit with no limits. So remain alert and watchful, ye of little circumspection, and take heed.

Beware the Jabberwock, my son!
The jaws that bite, the claws that catch!
Beware the Jubjub bird, and shun
The frumious Bandersnatch!

32

To Serve Man

Carpe diem appears to be dead (unless the new meaning is seize someone else's day, as a vicarious experience, of course — not hands-on or anything that dangerous). I say this because recently I was sitting in a restaurant where a young woman and some friends were celebrating her birthday. As they brought out the flaming cake and sang a rousing, albeit a bit slurred, rendition of *Happy Birthday*, she was more focused on recording it on her phone than "being in the moment," as they like to say.

But apparently, being in the moment is another anachronistic concept, gone along with *carpe diem* to the graveyard of all that is no longer in vogue or useful. Or safe for those of us interested in keeping life at arm's length. Better to stay in our snug and secure space than chance the slings and arrows of outrageous interpersonal contact.

Hey, life's hard — especially if you actually participate in it. Good news, though: Thanks to modern know-how, we no longer need anybody else to live vicariously. We can now live vicariously through ourselves, much like those worms that have both male and female sex organs and can reproduce without any help.

Way back in 1983, Billy Joel sang a prescient song titled *An Innocent Man* with the lyric, "Some people stay far away from the door if there's a chance of it opening up." It took a while, but we're becoming the embodiment of that rather trepidatious characterization, especially if you've reached adulthood in the early part of the 21st century (and you know who I mean).

I don't blame our current state of possible imminent collapse exclusively on computers and cell phones. On the contrary, I think the technology explosion is only a part of mankind's deconstruction of all that we used to cherish as independence and self-sufficiency. Regrettably, that old-time version of the romantic hero was not an equal-opportunity provider, and because some people succeeded and others failed, it wasn't fair.

OMG! Feelings were hurt!

I remember the two most emphatic precursors of that movement — they made the hairs on the back of my neck stand on end and clanged the fog bell of imminent foundering somewhere in the deep recesses of my primal awakening. I was coaching Little League baseball and attended a meeting of the organization's board where it was discussing buying chest protectors for every player to wear at all times during a game. You see, a young ball player in California had been hit in the chest by a pitched ball as he stood in the batter's box, and it killed him. The boy experienced ventricular fibrillation, caused by *commotio cordis*, a Latin medical term meaning agitation of the heart, which can cause ventricular fibrillation and sudden death. However, as scary as the incident was, it's about as rare as a bridge collapsing because of resonant frequency.

But thanks to our ever-vigilant media for their dependable hysterical overreaction that helps sell cottony-smooth toilet paper and miracle creams to help stamp out, once and for all, the heartbreak of psoriasis, a movement began. Since it wasn't practical to cover all the kids in bubble wrap, the ridiculous, expensive and constricting chest protectors became the latest *cause célèbre*. I know, I know, it's for the kids' safety. After all, our kids are delicate china dolls, made of brittle porcelain, right? Precious, dear little artifacts of untold worth because, let's face it, nobody ever took child-rearing as seriously as we do or invested as much money into the project. Right?

I mean, we're right, right?

Yeah, we understand that kids die, but we want that to happen no more, so we're doing something about it, and by God, you better make it so or we'll hold our breath until we turn blue. Or march with vulgar signs and shrill voices raised in a cacophony of overcompensation. Forget the unpleasant truth that we're raising generations of ineffectual, namby-pamby, mollycoddled, delicate, self-absorbed and lifelong appurtenances to mommy and daddy (and their surrogates); we're busy changing the world and one must make sacrifices.

Such as self-esteem. Or self-reliance. Or any sense of self at all.

Which those of us who came of age in the 20th century obtained on the playground and in our backyard through the time-honored tradition of natural selection. Hold on Hercules, Beowulf and Karna, we don't roll that way in the age of vicarious. Where you used to learn and sharpen your life skills by dealing with bullies and disparities in ability and opportunity, we no longer tolerate those obstacles. No child left behind, and all that. Except bullies, of course. We don't care for bullies, unless we must bully in the name of righteousness and self-actualization. (There are all kinds of bullying, aren't there?)

To hell with DNA and eons of learned behavior ...

... like a boy I know who found out the hard way. His name is Cyrus and he's a tough kid who could easily be labeled a bully by today's standards. In my youth, he would've been considered just another boy who stood up for himself, which is no longer acceptable behavior, as he was to learn. At school, a bigger boy took a swing at him, so Cyrus swung back and beat the snot out of the bigger boy. Cyrus received a week's suspension for protecting himself. The principal explained that it was wrong to fight back, that Cyrus should have turtled and waited for help to arrive.

OMG redux.

And you wonder why this generation is ultra-sensitive, easily distracted and unable to deal maturely with disapproval and failure: they never learned how — they're being raised by a cadre of Neville Chamberlains. Nor are they being challenged by the difficult realities of life, like the presumed uber-fragile students of a certain eastern Pennsylvania school district. During a recent cold snap of single-digit temperatures, the superintendent closed all the schools because ... well ... he didn't want the kids to get cold.

I kid you not!

In justifying the closings for three days, he said, "We have to be sensitive to the babies who are walking outside." (He actually used those words.)

OMG squared to the gazillionth power! And guess what many of those babies did during that unscheduled three-day holiday? You guessed it: They went skiing and sledding and skating, or spent the day outside playing in the snow (those who knew how to participate in activities that required more coordination than rapid thumb movement, that is).

There's not enough bubble wrap in the world to fix that kind of assumptive conceit. And the lessons learned are incalculable in terms of self-worth and entitlement. So, if you get a bad grade, go to the board of education. If you don't make the team, sue. If you don't get the job, file a complaint with the EEOC. If your candidate doesn't win, cry and stomp your feet and act like a wild bunch of jejune jackanapes.

I don't assign this behavior exclusively to millennials, and not all millennials are like this. As a matter of fact, many aren't, and many longer-in-the-tooth adults are just as caught up in the trend of superficial, derivative identity. I'm not only talking about generational millennials here, but a broader swath of our society that has glommed onto the trophy babies' mentality, who are fixated on shallow, egotistical validations through external, extrinsic values such as money, notoriety and image, and much less concerned with more meaningful, intrinsic values such as self-acceptance, civility, tolerance and community.

Unfortunately, we currently find ourselves in a caviling sea of narcissistic lollygagging without a paddle or sail or even a boat. And all the carping, feet-stomping, bellyacher-zealots are being led by a bunch of Captain Ahabs, determined to chase the ostensibly elusive yet remarkably unattainable unequivocal truth — the great white whale of subterfuge, exclusively for the benefit of all those emotionally peg-legged, monomaniacal self-pursuers, the shallowest segments of our society: politicians, aided by their first-mate enablers, the media and entertainers — our fearless defenders of all that's self-serving, the bastion of selfish petulance, the last guard of "I got mine and I don't really care if you get yours, but I'll carry and wave that banner as long as you keep me out front and away from the maddening crowd (because let's be real: You're all deplorables to us — an inconvenient truth)."

The calamitous result of these autocratic bloodsuckers' unquenchable avarice is the spawning of a multitude of ill-informed and compliant golems, nurtured and trained to support even the most outrageous nonsense. This malevolent construct is no accident, no fluke of nature; it's a plan designed to keep the rich and powerful rich and powerful. The first pragmatic manifestation of this Machiavellian concept for group brainwashing appeared in *Mein Kampf*, written by Adolf Hitler while he was in prison after World War I, and universally identified as the Big Lie. Joseph Goebbels, Hitler's minister of propaganda, took it even further when he wrote: "The essential English leadership secret does not depend on particular intelligence. Rather, it depends on a remarkably stupid thick-headedness. The English follow the principle that when one lies, one should lie big, and stick to it. They keep up their lies, even at the risk of looking ridiculous."

Stupid is as stupid does, and we be doing lots o' stupid.

As we're being taught in our complicit education systems because, as I'm sure you know, it takes a village to effectively brainwash enough of us to support such a simple, albeit devious and amoral concept: Make the lie big enough and repeat it often enough and it will become fact to the great (intellectually unsophisticated and nincompoopedly trusting) unwashed.

That's us, folks!

Now, you on the left are saying to yourselves, "By Jove, you nailed those rascally Republicans on that one," while you on the right are all, "Golly gee, that's a damned sound definition of all those deceitful Democrats."

Congratulations — you've just personified the purpose of the Big Lie: Keep the proletariat divided, pissed off and distracted while we continue to pick their pockets and steal their faith and their will. In other words, they don't care what side you're on or what you believe as long as you're thoroughly caught up in pursuing red herrings and not watching them; keep your eye on the mesmerizing bouncing ball and forget about my other hand, boys and girls.

Don't wanna be an American idiot, one nation controlled by the media. Information Age of hysteria, it's calling out to idiot America.

Most of the insipid empty shirts we send to Washington these days are a far cry from what the Founding Fathers had in mind. They envisioned people taking time out of their lives to serve, then returning to their farms, factories, shops or jobs, many of whom left George Washington's ("I've got a bridge to sell you") swamplands broke or nearly broke.

Ha! What imponderous fools. Today, being elected to office is your ticket to wealth, guileful influence and free and lavish lifelong benefits. It's better than playing the lottery because it's a sure thing: You get to call the shots and vote yourself anything you please, as you razzle-dazzle 'em with exploitive rhetoric and an unscrupulous deportment fit for the finest reprobates we have to offer.

You dad gum guv'ment, you sorry rakafratchits. You got yourself an itch and you want me to scratch it.

Hey, I'm not making this stuff up. The late Lee Iacocca said pretty much the same thing about our current leadership: "Am I the only guy in this country who's fed up with what's happening? Where the hell is our outrage? We should be screaming bloody murder. We've got a gang of clueless bozos steering our ship of state right over a cliff, we've got corporate gangsters stealing us blind, and we can't even clean up after a hurricane, much less build a hybrid car. But instead of getting mad, everyone sits around and nods their heads when the politicians say, 'Stay the course.' Stay the course? You've got to be kidding. This is America, not the damned Titanic. I'll give you a sound bite: Throw the bums out!"

Stay the course, of course, means keep electing me, and what better way to keep yourself ensconced in the good life with your year-round climate-controlled mansions and big, gas-guzzling SUVs to transport your armed security detail and your private jets and yachts and your privileged, gated communities than by creating a generation of non-participants, a host of anxiety-ridden, ineffectual dependents willing to surrender their self-sufficiency and sit on the sidelines to root for their team and throw rocks and bottles and marinate in the pure, autogenic hate that fires the engine that makes this all possible, *cause fire is the devil's only friend.*

Today's Big Lies, and they're coming at us fast and furious, are being proffered by the deceitful, despotic, demented dynasts to promote their own welfare to the exclusion of the people who support their egocentric efforts — beyond a riddle wrapped in a mystery inside an enigma, it's the ultimate manipulation of inherent insecurities promoted and exploited by the new masters and mistresses of the universe, the otherwise useless appendages that hang inefficaciously like an infected appendix, covertly sucking the life out of the body whole as it slowly kills it. Reminds me of an episode of *The Twilight Zone* about the Kanamits, a giant alien race that came to Earth to ostensibly help and promote the welfare of mankind. They brought along a book titled *To Serve Man.* After spending some time helping the unsuspecting earthlings with all manner of societal improvements, the good people of Earth line up to visit the Kanamits' home planet, blasting off into outer space with smiles on their faces and songs in their hearts. Unfortunately for the gullible and unsuspecting carbon-based bipeds, *To Serve Man* turns out to be a cookbook.

And how do you suppose you'll be served: rare, medium or well done? It doesn't really matter what repast you become because we're all consumable commodities to the overlords — the dragon-willers and malevolent beheaders in our very real game of thrones. So, before you become a crispy critter or lose your head, take heed: The world is not your oyster unless you're willing to go digging with all the inherent risks of getting wet, cold or being eaten by the cleverest of all sharks. And it's especially not okay to forgo oysters simply because you're afraid. We're all afraid — life is scary, like a roller coaster or watching *Keeping Up with the Kardashians*. To live, to really live, is to face those fears, *to take arms against a sea of troubles, and by opposing end them.*

But we don't do that, do we? Oh no, we continue to pretend to have relationships via Twitter and Instagram, and whenever we're forced to actually meet up, we hug and kiss like there's no tomorrow because if we're hugging and kissing so much, we must be fully engaged and really, really good people, even though that engagement includes keeping those ubiquitous screens pasted in front of our faces because, like, we really, really care about you and all, but, you know, we don't want to miss anything happening that might actually bring some true meaning to our overly connected, yet incredibly disassociated lives.

And we'll post and paste our group-approved judgmental opinions and clever memes, totally lacking in any original thought or accountability because, well, it's important, like, you know, to say and write stuff that's superficial and tediously predictable because, gee willikers, nobody likes a smart aleck and, wow, that could be like, you know, really, abusive behavior to totally disagree with somebody who's not entirely frabernackle.

And we'll buy jeans with holes in them and pay through the

nose to look like what used to be called hobos; wear clothes that don't fit and waste a good deal of our time and energy pulling and tugging and adjusting; grow long beards and shave our heads in an asymmetry that appropriately reflects the asymmetry of our collective confusion; decorate our bodies with images and symbols that are supposed to reveal our true inner souls — our individuality — but in reality are just another plaintive cry for inclusion, a desperate need to count.

Ah yes, the millennials, Generation Y, Generation WE, The Boomerang Generation (because they have a tendency to move back home with their parents), The Peter Pan Generation (because they shun responsibility) — lots of unflattering monikers for a curious sociological group spawned in the residual fallout of the technological revolution, dust-of-the-earth manifestations of complex programming languages and miraculous microprocessors, here to usher in the latest frontier, self-possessed guides to the new order, void of obsolete conceptualizations such as privacy or singular uniqueness or risk/reward. And nowhere is that sociological distinction more prevalent than in today's workplace, where according to Sally Kane at thebalancecareers.com, millennials crave attention. She writes that they seek "feedback and guidance and appreciate being kept in the loop and often need frequent praise and reassurance. Millennials may benefit greatly from mentors who can help guide and develop their talents. This is where the boomers come in handy because (though mostly retired), they have something to offer and see mentoring millennials as one way they can continue to contribute to the workforce."

And *voilà*, or as Andy Kaufman might have put it, *here I come to save the day*, a bonified, genuine baby boomer (mostly unretired) to offer a bit of wisdom and a touch of avuncular guidance to all you fledgling abecedarians. As you might expect, millennials are the fastest-growing segment of the workforce, and as employers compete for their talents, the group's distinctive and idiosyncratic characteristics are becoming harder and harder to disregard. Companies can no longer ignore the needs, desires and attitudes of this large and demanding generation that has come to be defined by a perplexing set of personality traits. Here are a few of those perplexing traits and advice from my distinctive and idiosyncratic perspective:

Millennials Need Instant Gratification: Instant gratification is a myth. It doesn't exist. Get over it. What comes easy, goes easy and has no real value to begin with.

It don't come easy; you know it don't come easy.

There are no participation trophies out here in the terrifying jungle of humanity, so stop expecting people to give a damn about you just because you showed up. Showing up may be a big part of success, but you need to bring with you something more than a quizzical smile and neat-o 'do. Unfortunately, your sense of self has been all tied up in group identity — that's how you've been taught — but out here in the cold, hard world, and in spite of what the puppeteers say to keep you divided and comfortable in your odious outrage, most people don't care if you're male or female, black or white, where you were born, who you sleep with, who you worship or who's your daddy, just what can you do for them. Accordingly, you should be more focused on who you are rather than what you are, so please resist the unrelentingly reinforced notion that you are special. You are not.

Millennials Think They're Special: Being special is a myth. It doesn't exist. Get over it. This popular notion that everybody is born special is pure poppycock. Special is not given; special is earned. If you want to be special, a truly special person, then don't follow the well-worn path of conformity, of fear-based living. Oh sure, we're all special to our families, our friends, our lovers (well, most of us are), but, generally speaking, that's a biological reaction, an unregulated electronic impulse emanating from the brain, programmed into our systems by millennia of fighting the harsh realities of protection and fortification against the ever-changing machine of life. Rage against the machine! Don't be like:

> *Welcome my son, welcome to the machine.*
> *Where have you been?*
> *It's alright we know where you've been.*
> *You've been in the pipeline, filling in time.*

Be more like:

> *We need a movement with a quickness.*
> *You are a witness of change.*
> *And to counteract,*
> *We gotta take the power back.*

But that's not easy to do, and they sure as hell don't want you kicking up any dust or peeking at the man behind the curtain. That kind of dangerous attitude is heresy in the ongoing war for the ultimate control of your mind and soul. They desperately need you to believe you are special, and that it's them (the machinees), and only them (the corrupt, devious, inglorious bastard machinees) that make it so. So, *rage, rage against the dying of the light,* and *do not go gentle into that good night.* (Lots of nifty quotes to Google while spending quality time with your BFF.)

Or maybe that's all too much and you just want to go on thinking you're special. Okay then:

> *You are a fluke of the universe.*
> *You have no right to be here.*
> *And whether you can hear it or not,*
> *The universe is laughing behind your back.*

<u>Millennials are Multitaskers</u>: Multitasking is a myth. It doesn't exist. Get over it. Oh, I get it: You're the superhuman generation that can do it all, harness technology and use it as your bitch. Well guess what? *The bitch is back* ... and she's

pissed off! To begin, technology is a tool, not a reflection of who you are. Unfortunately, it's being used more as a disguise, a distorted mirror of who you think you are or who you'd like to be; a mask, something to hide behind, to protect you from being discovered for the freighted fraud, the compliant charlatan you may very well be.

Throw 'em a fake and a finaqle. They'll never know you're just a bagel.

Please get this through your pointy little heads: THERE'S NO SUCH THING AS MULTITASKING! (And yes, I'm shouting.) Can't be done. You're either doing one thing or another, and if you're trying to do two things at the same time, you're doing them both poorly. Period. End of story. And here's why: Regardless of all the empty platitudes and cute *bon mots*, you have only 100 percent to give. There is no 110 percent or any other sophistic deviation from the laws of math that apply — only 100 percent of your time and concentration is available. So, if you're trying to do multiple tasks, you are only giving some of yourself to each of them and cheating each of them of the rest of you. In other words, you're doing a half-assed job on everything. Keep that up and it won't be all:

> *You're my end and my beginning.*
> *Even when I lose I'm winning*
> *'Cause I give you all, all of me.*

It is often said (usually by millennials) that millennials are multitasking pros and can juggle many responsibilities at once.

Pure unadulterated hogwash!

What it really means is that you are easily distracted and find social media and messaging hard to resist. In other words, we've weaned a gaggle of electronic junkies who can't focus on any given, single task. Sure, you can ride your bike and use your phone, you can run and use your phone, you can work out and use your phone, you can send emails and post really cool memes and use other functions of your phone at the same time, you can chew gum and talk on your phone, you can be in a face-to-face conversion with a viable, breathing human being and use your phone, and I assume you can have sex (with a viable, breathing human being, hopefully) while using your phone, but you cannot — no way, no how — live your life to the fullest, exist on the edge of uncontaminated enlightenment, suck every ounce of nectar from the sweet fruit of being, smell the roses or shout out *I am I cried, I am said I* while using your phone.

Turn it off and tune in. It's not as scary as you think. Honest.

<u>Millennials Want Balance in Their Lives:</u> Balance in life is a myth. It doesn't exist. Get over it. Unlike generations before you, you seem unwilling to sacrifice your personal lives to benefit your career. You appear to believe that playing hard is more important than working hard, and you seemingly have the misguided impression that work is supposed to be fun.

Fun? They call it work, remember? That's for a reason: It's work. Fun is a three-letter word that backwards spells 'nuf' — which has no meaning, which is the same value fun has to the job. Workplace fun is an oxymoron, morons and moronettes. FYI, an oxymoron is combining two words with opposite meanings to create a desired effect, and in this case the effect is, "Are you freaking kidding me?"

Yes, your job should be rewarding, should be fulfilling, should be satisfying, but fun is what you do on Saturday night at Skate-a-Rama with *Sloppy Sue and Big Bone Billy*. Don't confuse happiness with fun, or pleasure. As Margaret Paul writes at huffpost.com, "We are a pleasure-seeking society. Most of us spend our energy seeking pleasure and avoiding pain. We hope that by doing this, we will feel happy. Yet deep, abiding happiness and joy elude so many people." That's because we tend to confuse the two concepts, especially those of instant gratification orientation. Pleasure is a temporary feeling that comes from external stimuli: a good meal, an enjoyable movie, executing the perfect travailing toe pivot with Sloppy Sue, making love while not on the phone, etc.

Happiness, on the other hand, is internal and comes from being connected to yourself.

Don't panic — you won't find an app for that on your phone. But there is an icon embedded in your internal system, deep down inside, and all you need to do is find it. It's there you'll discover the fulfillment you seek (and nowhere else). As you begin this amazing journey, though, please keep in mind this truism: Life is not fair, and good luck with that balance thing:

Get over it, get over it.
All this whinin' and cryin' and pitchin' a fit,
Get over it, get over it.

Millennials Want to be Equal: Equality is a myth. It doesn't exist. Get over it. You may be equal in the eyes of the Lord, but here on terra firma, you ain't jack, Jack and Jackettes, at least not until you've paid your dues. Regrettably, you've been led to believe that you can accomplish anything you set your mind on. Oh, okay: Please let me know when you harness that positive energy enough to jump over the Empire State Building — that I want to see. Truth is, you can accomplish many things in life if you're willing to work hard, but you have limitations. Sorry to burst your bubble, but learning to accept those limitations and concentrate on your strengths is a tough bucket of nails, especially when you've been coddled and propped up all through your formal schooling.

Yeah, yeah, yeah, you're such a gifted generation of brainiacs that your elementary school eschewed structured grades and used only passive recognition on your report cards, such as "Satisfactory" or "Unsatisfactory" instead of letter grades, along with appropriate comments such as "Well Done" or "Good Job" or "Nice Work" except the one time a teacher wrote, "Great Effort" and your mom and dad had to go down to the school to set that teacher straight by reminding her that "Great Effort" means you failed but really tried and that kind of passive-aggressive patronizing of such an obviously and extremely gifted child is completely unacceptable and you never got a comment like that one again, for sure, because, let's be clear here, you're the most gifted, special, extraordinary example of homo-erectus-ascending ever erected.

Congratulation on that erection. However, the true equation for success in life is really rather uncomplicated: No one is going to treat you as an equal, appreciate your talents and efforts, empower you, legitimize you, liberate you, enthuse you or disabuse you until you see yourself as equal, appreciate your own talents and efforts, empower yourself, legitimize yourself, liberate yourself, enthuse yourself and disabuse yourself first. When it comes to establishing your place in the world, you are the alpha and the omega, the yin and the yang, the be all and end all, the boss with the sauce, the last word — it's all about you (just as you suspected all along): the good and bad, the successes and failures, the pleasures and frustrations, all up to you.

But there is one thing holding you back. The obvious and over-messaged response to that statement, of course — the one you've heard so many times it's become a cliché — is you. But I'm afraid it lies much deeper than that perfunctory answer, somewhere in the safest recesses of your tattered psyche, a secret place you keep hidden from the world, the real you, the one you know best, the one that makes you feel inadequate and unlovable because that's exactly what dependency does to people: It teaches them that they're not capable of taking care of themselves, that they're inadequate, unworthy, a burden, and those feelings inevitably lead to self-loathing.

Where do you think all this hate comes from? It sure doesn't come from nowhere. No, no Nanette, it starts with you and how you feel about yourself. It's as simple as that: Fix the way you feel about yourself and cure the world of hate (at least your world). You better, seriously, because hate doesn't destroy the other guy; it destroys you.

But how do you do that? Well, it takes some real effort and

applied disciplines to slay the mightiest dragon of them all, the one that lives inside your barely penetrated cranium, stirring up all the head trash it can lay its crooked, sticky fingers on. Step one in the crusade: Watch *She's Out of My League*. The movie stars Jay Baruchel as Kirk who meets a beautiful young woman named Molly, played by Alice Eve. Kirk's buddy, Stainer, played by T.J. Miller, labels her a solid 10, and Kirk an arguable five. No chance for Kirk in this mismatch, right? We're talking Hollywood here, babes. The central problem of the movie is that Kirk believes he is a five, and because of that, Molly is unattainable, and as long as he believes he is a five, she is. *(Whether you think you can, or whether you think you can't, you're right.)* These guys have spent their entire lives rating people on a system based solely on external characteristics, and after the predictable trials and tribulations of young love, both Kirk and Stainer come to realize that it's what's inside a person that counts; that who you are is more important than what you are. With that hard-earned knowledge and the conviction of his newfound inner strength, we see Kirk and Molly flying into the sunset together forever (which by Hollywood standards means about as long as it takes for the ink on the prenup to dry).

Once you get past the obligatory profanity (because you millennials, apparently, love the f-bomb ... and blowing up stuff) and the superfluous scatology, it's a good movie with an important and timeless message. Whoever you want to be, you already are. You just need to find it. And that's been no easy task for you millennials. I thought my grandmother's generation had it rough with all the monumental changes during their lives — going from no conveniences to electricity, telephones, washing machines, refrigerators, movies, radio, television, cars, jet planes, space travel — but you guys trump that in spades. You're the first generation that had to deal with the daunting burden of having the entirety of mankind's accumulated knowledge at your beck and call, and the utility to instantly communicate with the entire world.

Wow!

That's overwhelming and an awesome weight of power to carry around on your shoulders. No wonder you equate external connections with being in touch with yourself, and no wonder you're so overstimulated and hypersensitive. Like right now, I bet you think I hate you. I don't. (I have a plethora of millennial progeny, being not just a wise old soul but a prolific one, as well.) You may think I hate you because hate is an essential operative construct in today's abstract conceptual emotions. But hate is not an emotion. It's a reaction, a direct result of fear. Unfortunately, fear drives most of our actions. Being afraid is not a weakness, but letting fear rule your life is:

> Got to pull myself together
> I don't want to die of fright
> What can I do to keep from going
> Crazy in the night

The best way to combat fear and all its debilitating manifestations is to engage fully. Join your life copiously and repulse those trying to control it. My final advice is to listen to The Who's *Baba O'Riley*, but if that's too esoteric for you, go with Funkadelic: *Shit, goddamn, get off your ass and jam.* Too urban? Then try one of your faves, J.K. Rowling: "It is impossible to live without failing at something, unless you live so cautiously that you might as well not have lived at all — in which case, you fail by default."

That's right, dudes and dudettes, life can be hard, very, very hard, but even harder when you try to hide from it. Truth be told, you can't hide from it because it will eventually come and get you. Like growing old: It's inevitable. You may think you have it schussed, but you're only fooling yourselves. So stop fooling yourself — seize the day, stay in the moment, *and when you get the choice to sit it out or dance, I hope you dance.*

33

To Be or Not to Be, That is the Question

Did you hear the one about the contractor who died and went to the possibly sacred, possibly secular, maybe nonexistent or with streets-paved-of-gold place you go when you die?

When he got to the reputedly gated entrance to the possibly sacred, possibly secular, maybe nonexistent or with streets-paved-of-gold place you go when you die, he was greeted by a disembodied voice or a winged elderly person or an unidentified manifestation of the great void, that welcomed and congratulated him on living to be 126 years old.

"What are you talking about?" he asked the disembodied voice or the winged elderly person or an unidentified manifestation of the great void. "I'm 45 years old. Why do you think I'm 126?"

"Because we added up your time sheets!" was the reply from said possibilities.

I know, a long way to go for a weak payoff, but you get my point.

Contractors have a dubious reputation because people fear being ripped off by them. They fear being ripped off by them because they don't fully understand what most contractors do. That's because contractors have done a pretty bad job of selling themselves.

That's right: It all comes back to sales.

Throughout the post-World War II era of prosperity, when you couldn't build, fix, improve and replace things in or about your domicile quickly enough, contractors had it relatively easy when it came to selling their services. But then came the great enlightenment, when we discovered that rich investment bankers (enabled by their political sycophantic sidekicks) are generally greedy, myopic, underhanded, self-worshipping, avaricious, greedy and downright not-nice megalomaniacs who would gladly destroy an economy or two for an extra billion stuffed away in the old mattress (more commonly known as "what once was ours").

And wham, just like that, in the flick of a flicker, in the whisp of a whisper, it was all gone. Reality reared its ugly head and everybody could see that the emperor was, indeed, quite naked. And along with that painful correction of misguided faith and belief, many contractors were looking down the steely double barrels of a 12-gauge, Dodo-bird disappearing act.

Hocus pocus, alakazam, gone in a puff of immolated smoke was the booming construction business' easy money.

Now you see me, now you don't was the painful lament of the real estate market, a dependable contributory to the building industry's copious green stream.

Goodbye cruel world, I'm off to join the circus was the strangled cry of mortgage companies throughout the land as the abundant funding tap dwindled down to a trickle, leaving those new builds and home improvement projects on the planning board.

But not all contractors suffered to the same degree. The smart ones, the ones who understood that they sell more than plumbing or heating or roofing or new-home construction, are still very much alive and kicking and padding their time sheets. They're still very much alive and kicking and padding their time sheets because they know that customers don't care as much about the great features of their work as they care about the benefits.

What's in it for me?

And that's one of the most basic tenets of sales.

In other words, the astute and the perceptive (the contractors who survived and thrived), learned how to sell their product using a skilled, professional sales approach. And that approach is only available to those willing to invest a bit of time and money, and willing to suspend a belief system normally resistant to change.

To be more than they are.

To be successful.

So, if you want to sell more — of anything — learn more about how to do it. It's really that simple. And the next time the chewing gum and chicken wire-wielding magicians who dominate and manipulate the fragile house of cards we like to call our financial infrastructure come calling, hat in hand, you'll be much better prepared *to strive with difficulties, and to conquer them,* which is what Samuel Johnson called *the highest human fancily.*

34

Tattoos of Memories and
Dead Skin on Trial

"What's a loofah?" I asked my wife one morning.

"Epidermal sandpaper," she replied. "It exfoliates your skin — gets rid of dead cells."

"Exfoliates? I thought that's why I showered twice a day."

No, I'm not a germaphobe, I'm an oldmanaphobe — I don't want to get old and have to endure all the attendant degradation. (Why do we cherish everything old — wine, whiskey, cheese, art, music, literature, handcrafted furniture, cars, historical buildings, vintage clothing, even trees — everything but people?) So in my quest to remain in good standing with the Pepsi Generation (or is it the Tide-Pod generation) and stay fit and fresh, I go to the gym in the morning and shower before work, then I ride my bike (the kind you pedal, not the kind you sublimate with) later in the day and shower before dinner. And I'm a very good showerer, so I can't imagine leaving much dermatological debris behind.

Ha! Little did I know what kind of hideous decomposition I was hosting.

It all started with a harmless conversation I had with a young lady at the gym about skin care, for reasons that now escape me (but probably had something to do with her yoga pants). She was vigorously tattooed, so I guessed that care of skin was one of her sweet spots.

She told me I should loofah.

"What's that?" I asked. "A new dance?"

"You're funny," she said, and danced her yoga pants back to

operatur ad perfectionem.

As a consequence of that brief confabulation, I ended up learning quite a bit about dead skin and exfoliating ... on the internet. I had no choice. I visited a drugstore, a health store and a big box store that specializes in kitchen and bathroom things, but could find no one to educate me on the benefits of loofahing, other than "it removes dead skin and it's good for you."

Okay, got that. But why is it good for me and how much dead skin do I have and why do I have to remove it and what are the benefits of removing it and what happens if I don't remove it and will it make me look 30 again?

Which goes a long way in explaining the demise of retail.

I know, I know, it's the big bad internet.

Just like newspapers that were rolling along, singing a song until the World Wide Web reared its ugly head and rendered The Fourth Estate as irrelevant as men's suits that fit. Yes, the internet has created a whole new marketplace — rearranged the furniture, so to speak. And although it has changed the rules, retail and newspapers put up about as much resistance as Old Bill Sherman faced marching through the dispirited and defeated South.

They weren't beaten; they quit.

And the weapon of choice was greed: my greed, your greed, our greed.

It used to be that a person opened a business to earn an honest living, make enough to provide for his family and pay his employees and suppliers. Then the money changers showed up and all bets were off. They realized that great profits could be made by charging higher prices, paying employees less and utilizing more efficient (read cheaper) material and systems. Wall Street was born and peace on Earth, goodwill toward men became it's a dog-eat-dog world and we're all wearing Milk-Bone underwear. Ah, but these boys were smart and knew they couldn't keep making obscene profits if they didn't cut us in, allow us to dip our beaks for a small taste. And *voilà*, 401Ks and

IRAs, the most beautiful example of coerced collusion that ever came out of the devil's workshop (found in Lower Manhattan not too far from the fish markets that actually make the air around the center of commerce smell better).

Not too long ago, cities and towns throughout the land were chock full of small, mom-and-pop stores providing goods and services while operating profitably. But none of those store owners had places in the Hamptons or private jets to get there, so Corporate America stepped in to show them the error of their ways. The good folks at Corporate America did this by putting most of them out of business, moving massive retail outlets of all stripes into the hamlets and conurbations and dropping prices until the smaller retailers couldn't compete. Then, naturally, they raised prices and cut costs, and everybody's investment accounts grew.

Yay!

The axis of the world tilted toward rapacious opulence and it was no longer good enough to make money; you now had to make lots of money. It's the piggy effect, and guess who those piggies are?

Oink, oink!

And then along comes Al Gore to invent the internet, and poof! profits suffered. Instead of realizing the golden goose had crapped out and making adjustments in their business plans and expectations, the Main-Street-killers attempted to compete on the internet's terms, which of course, was impossible — like bringing a knife to a .50-caliber machine gun fight. Rather than accept smaller quarterly projections and operate their businesses on a lower profit margin while staying in business and providing all the associated communal benefits, our collective greed dictated a cut-and-run maneuver.

Goodbye traditional retail and hello to buying things online that are the wrong color or don't fit and it takes a degree from MIT to figure out the labyrinthian return policy. One giant step for avaricious, trepidatious wussyism; one small step for all that dead skin hitching a ride on my otherwise scrubbed and virtuous hide. All because we collectively bow down to the most sacred of all gods: money. Forget the fat cats in their Bentleys and Maseratis, we of the great unwashed love to sit back and watch our mutual funds spinning like a casino slot machine, licking our chops and living day to day in anticipation of pre-end-of-life indolence, while complaining about the money grubbers who close businesses and lay off our friends and neighbors. In truth, the only difference between greedy rich people and greedy poor people is that greedy rich people are better at it.

The great irony here is that the world of retail is now caught in a death spiral of the new circle of life. Barnes & Noble, one of the most aggressive and successful acquisitive boll weevils, spent decades acquiring and shutting down independent bookstores until it was practically the only game in town. Then Amazon reinvented the book-selling industry, leaving B&N scrambling to protect its market share, any market share. But what goes around comes around, and eventually B&N couldn't compete and profits plummeted, as the once-darling of Wall Street became *persona non grata* at the chic cocktail parties on the South Fork of Long Island. B&N ended up being dumped onto one of the bottom feeders of the stock market's wheel of fortune, a hedge fund, that will most assuredly conduct massive layoffs and selloffs, disrupting and dismantling the lives of thousands of loyal employees without so much as a "Howdy do, Harry."

An old aphorism asserts that retail is detail, and we all know that the devil is in the details. So, if you find yourself stuck in the middle of a loofah nightmare like I did, don't be too quick to blast external forces for your dilemma. Take a beat and consider your own culpability, and remember what the Rolling Stones sang in one of their more lucid moments: *I shouted out "Who killed the Kennedys?" When after all, it was you and me.*

Postscript: If you're wondering what I learned about loofahing, it's complicated. One source says it's beneficial because it removes dead cells, allowing more oxygen to reach the new cells and invigorating healthy skin growth; while another source says it breaks down the natural barriers of protection that the epidermis maintains, exposing you to lots of potential infections and other bad stuff; and yet a third source says that loofahs are disgusting breeding grounds for all sorts of sleazy bacteria. I'm going with Yoga Pants on this one. She may not know much, but who cares.

35

Total Eclipse of the Brain

There's a scene from the 1996 movie *Independence Day* where people gather on top of the U.S. Bank Tower in Los Angeles to welcome the aliens, carrying signs and going all bananas over the really cool happening, until they are summarily zapped to smithereens by the indifferent extraterrestrials.

Reminds me of the solar eclipse in 2017, sans the complete annihilation of most living things.

You can understand the lemming-like, doltish conduct of the folks in *Independence Day* because they're from La La Land, but here in real America — everywhere that's not New York City or California — you'd expect more.

Like rational behavior.

I mean, it was an eclipse, not the second coming, for chrissakes. The media, as usual, obsessed over a rather commonplace, mundane event, whipping the validation-starved populace into a lather with dire warnings and euphoric promises of spiritual enlightenment. It seems as if the entire country was gaga over two ancient, celestial rocks, one cold and inert, the other on fire, passing by each other.

Big whoop!

It happens two to five times a year, folks. This momentous, historic event has occurred billions and billions of times before. That's more times than Madonna's been kissed, more times than Ben Affleck's made a bad movie, even more times than Chris Christie's eaten a donut (but not by much).

In the hysteria, we were incessantly warned not to look at the sun.

Really?

Oh, but Mama, that's where the fun is.

And the dogs! My God, the dogs! Whatever you do (when you're not busy not staring at the sun), don't let your dog out or he could go blind!

Oh, the humanity ... er ... Oh, the caninanity!

I was driving during the big event and barely noticed it, while Peggy Lee plaintively sang in my head, "Is that all there is?"

So here's a clue: Next time you want to see a darkened sky in the middle of the day, run outside during a thunderstorm. You won't need any protective eyewear to look up at the lightning bolts or cumulonimbus clouds, and you'll have no trouble finding a good vantage point.

And don't forget your galoshes.

Such is America in the new millennium.

Okay, it was an interesting event and fun to be part of, I'm sure, just like when I was a kid. Back then, before the 24/7 news cycle, an eclipse was reported in the limited media we had available, and we would study the approaching spectacle in school. But on the big day, it was just a bunch of kids in the schoolyard looking through cereal boxes. Most grownups paid it little mind, and as soon as it was over, we went back to playing dodge ball and sucking on lead-based paint chips.

Ah, the good old days.

But nothing is that simple anymore. Living out here on the new frontier and trying to grapple with the ever-decreasing face-to-face, life-affirming access to fellow travelers on this amazing journey, any hint of common ground is like Dr Pepper to a hypoglycemic.

I just want something to hold on to, and a little of that human touch (two Springsteen quotes in one piece — my my).

In this edition of the human race, the descendants of Homo erectus have stumbled in the starting blocks (bent and crumpled over insidious machines of menticide and rapidly reducing millennia of learning how to stand up straight). We barely made it out of the Industrial Revolution and along comes the Information Age to smack us around for a while until we can learn to use information for something other than sharing embryotic, idiotic, commonly held misbeliefs and misguided insights of profound stupidity.

Other than that, we're doing fine.

The net result is that people have learned to deal primarily with external cause and effect, and spend little time on self-examination. So when a stupendously hyped external stimulus appears on the horizon, it's all hosanna in the highest.

"Finally, some substance and meaning to my life!"

Hardly.

The only true growth in life comes from the inside — from the internal struggle for self-awareness, behavioral modification and acceptance. No arbitrary heavenly manifestation or any other external experience can substitute for genuine introspection and personal development.

Like I run into every day.

There was a woman in one of my recent sales training classes who came to me after the fifth week and said, "I'm really disappointed. I thought you were going to teach us how to sell."

"That's what I'm trying to do," I responded.

"But all this psychological, self-analyzation stuff isn't what I was looking for."

"What is it you're looking for?" I asked.

"You know," she replied. "What to say to get people to do business with me."

"Oh," I answered. "You want the secret, magic words that automatically close sales. We don't get to those until week 10."

Then there was the business owner who hired me to help improve sales for his company. He paid me a lot of money and we spent a few sessions going over his organization and the systems and methods he used to run his sales team. He became very frustrated and finally burst out with, "Just tell me what to say!"

I sat there astonished. "What do you mean?" I asked.

"Just tell me what to say to my salespeople to get them to sell more," he practically screamed.

Both of these people were under the felonious impression that there is an enchanted formula floating around out there that shamans could teach them, amid burning incense and gentle background chimes, I'm sure.

Unfortunately, there is no esoteric, clandestine covenant of mystic sales trainers able to overcome weaknesses within you or your company by sprinkling a little fairy dust and whispering in your ear. Success comes from the inside, and the more you look outside, the harder it gets to unlock the inside.

But maybe you'll get lucky and find the guy selling those magic beans. Maybe you'll plant those beans and they'll grow into a giant bean stalk that you can climb and find the goose that lays the golden eggs. If you do, however, please take my advice: Don't let your goose look into the sun.

Oh, the goosanity!

36

Epilogue

There are lots of adjectives used these days by the media to describe our current state of affairs, but one you seldom hear is "hypocritical." That's because it's nearly impossible to see clearly through the sanctimonious prism of pious self-interest. But make no mistake, we 21st century voyagers live at the epicenter of unctuous, self-serving duplicity. In the pancake-makeup, hair-gel world of self-absorption, it's hard to discern when the talking heads are lying, but there is one sure way to know: Are their lips moving? (With apologies to lawyers everywhere.)

As I sat at my computer working on the last couple of pieces for this book, I was bombarded with hypocrisy from the unlimited sources at my disposal — the marvelous, algorithmic convention of instant inclusion that never stops working so effectively to separate us. First, I was hit with a few pop-ups about the latest mass shootings: 31 dead so far and dozens hurt during tandem acts of violence in another sad example of the alienation epidemic choking our country. My editor suggested I add "random" to "tandem," consistent with my fallow fatuous fondness for alliteration and homonyms, but there is nothing random about killing — it is most definitely deliberate and purposeful. We like to call these acts random because it alleviates a troubling sense of responsibility; we like to pretend they have nothing to do with us, that these events are otherworldly, outside our reality.

Until they happen to you, of course.

I got my information from a CNN article, and I had to scroll down several paragraphs to learn the details. That's because the story was mainly concerned with politicizing the horrific events.

So what else is new?

Thirty-one dead and the lead is all about how it's the other side's fault, the calamitous current currency of mass tragedy, the repugnant practice of using horrific events to personal advantage before the last shot is fired and the last victim hits the ground. During this same weekend, scores of people were shot in Chicago. The *Chicago Tribune* reported, "By Monday morning, 55 people had been shot across the city, seven of them fatally. The victims ranged from 5 to 56 years old." In a later edition, the paper reported that 309 people had been killed in Chicago by early August 2019 — 55 fewer than in all of 2018. But apparently that doesn't belong to all the news that's fit to print because hardly a peep was heard about it outside of Chicago.

You can bury your dead, but don't leave a trace. Hate your next-door neighbor, but don't forget to say grace. And you tell me over and over and over and over again my friend, you don't believe we're on the eve of destruction.

It was so disheartening to read all the undisguised hostility, the unbridled animosity, the pure hatred seething off of social media; disquieting anger that, completely unbeknownst to the obtuse keyboard pounders, fuels the engine that drives the fear that creates the hatred that provides the fuel they need to keep pounding the keyboard. It's a vicious cycle fed by our unscrupulous politicians and the sycophantic media. We're being led by some of the worst elements of our society, and we're all willing participants. As the old-time comic strip character Pogo put it many moons ago, "We have met the enemy and he is us."

You want to help stop this kind of madness? Then take the first step: Be nice to each other, even when you disagree. Really. I know it sounds simplistic and a bit naive, but try it ... please!

You and I must make a pact. We must bring salvation back.

In 1964, Marshall McLuhan coined the phrase "The medium is the message" in his book *Understanding Media: The Extensions of Man.* In a nutshell, he was commenting on how media (the vehicle) had become more important than the message (had become not only the vehicle, but the driver); how the media can control our thinking and behavior through the power of their influence. Boy, if McLuhan were alive today, he wouldn't have to roll over in his grave.

Ironically, as we've progressed through the variable manifestations of communication apparati, we've become much less communicative — at least, less effectively communicative. Oh, we communicate all the time, we communicate to death, but in all that chatter, we don't really say much. Unless, of course, you're a skilled politician, and in that case, you know how to lay your message in between the noise — you know how to deliver a subliminal message, even when you appear to be saying just the opposite.

Like a local congresswoman I know who posted a Father's Day message on Facebook. The message read, "Happy Good Guys Day to all the wonderful men out there who do so much for their children, their families, their communities, and the world. There is so much focus on women these days (not that I'm complaining), that I sometimes worry that we've lost sight of all the 'good guys' and their contributions to our society. So, Happy Good Guys Day! This includes all you dads who are celebrating your day!"

I have two things to say about that. The first thing: By saying there are good guys, it's implied that there are bad guys, so how do you decide who the good guys are? I mean, what are the criteria and who decides what the criteria are? It's all very confusing.

The second thing: Wouldn't it be insulting and cause some pretty significant outrage if a conservative, male congressman posted "Happy Good Gals Day" on Mother's Day? Wouldn't the folks out there who professionally deal in outrage find it condescending and sexist and maybe covertly predatory (you know, like one of those abstruse micro aggressions) for a man to judge women? Help me out here — I'm getting a headache!

And third (yes, third; I meant to say I have three things to say about that): Aren't we supposed to be all about inclusion? Did I miss a meeting?

And fourth (okay, I have four things to say — four — alright?): Gee, I hope I'm one of the good guys. Please let me know if I make the cut.

As you can see, hypocrisy can be subtle or in your face, like the uber-hypocrites who attended Google's July 2019 Davos-on-Sea climate change conclave, who were all over "Do as I say, not as I do." As Miranda Devine put it in the New York Post, "It doesn't get more hypocritical than A-listers jetting in on private planes to bemoan climate change at Google's private party in Sicily. The Gulfstreams, mega-yachts and gas-guzzling Maserati SUVs used to ferry the wokerati around the seaside Google Camp have been spewing out greenhouse gases at the rate of small nations."

She goes on to name some of the attendees: Barack Obama, Leonardo DiCaprio, Katy Perry, and my personal favorite, Prince Harry, who pledged to have only two children so as not to burden the world's already-taxed resources and further endanger the delicate balance of nature. What a guy, as he and the missus and their multiple attendants and entourage caravan in various modes of opulent transportation between one opulent palace to another opulent palace to other opulent domiciles with a deep and heavy conscience while "burning up more than 300 gallons of diesel an hour on their private yachts or spewing tons of CO_2 into the air from their private jets."

Thank God for Prince Harry and the other good guys.

Like the good guys at Sports Illustrated magazine, a forward-thinking publication that supports all kinds of populist objectives ... except when it comes to the objectification of women, and, in that case, not so much. Its annual swimsuit issue (soft porn, really) makes a ton of money for the titular titans of titties, and it's interesting that on Sixth

Avenue, much-maligned American capitalism still trumps political correctness.

To a point.

In the April 22-28, 2019, issue, SI highlighted quarterback Josh Rosen's pilgrimage to contemplate "his generation's responsibility to take care of the environment" ... in a behemoth RV that gets a whopping 10 miles per gallon. How's that for conscientious stewardship? And if you think the chutzpah can't get any deeper, there's an article in the same edition about how climate change is threatening sporting life in Canada and the northern United States. Maybe it's from all those colossal, confounded, carbon dioxide-spewing RVs?

Do you think?

There are all kinds of hypocrites in the world. Take Bernie Sanders ...

... please!

Sean Sullivan wrote in The Washington Post, "Sanders has made standing up for workers a central theme of his presidential campaign — this year marching with McDonald's employees seeking higher wages, pressing Walmart shareholders to pay workers more and showing solidarity with university personnel on strike. The independent from Vermont has proudly touted his campaign as the first presidential effort to unionize its employees, and his defense of the working class has been a signature element of his brand of democratic socialism and a rallying cry for the populist movement he claims to lead."

Unfortunately for Bernie, saying is easier than doing.

As it turns out, Sanders wasn't paying some of his campaign workers $15 an hour — one of the holy grails of his campaign and a weapon he has used tirelessly against his opponents. Sullivan added, "Campaign field hires have demanded an annual salary they say would be equivalent to a $15-an-hour wage, which Sanders for years has said should be the federal minimum. The organizers and other employees supporting them have invoked the senator's words and principles ..."

How did Sanders respond? Michael Knowles at Fox News reported, "Cowed by exposure in the media, Sanders finally relented and agreed to give his staffers what they want. But nothing comes without a price, and as Sanders announced the new minimum wage for field organizers, he simultaneously cut the total number of hours per week they can work. Not only will the organizers not earn more money, but they'll also lose valuable face time with the candidate and his more senior staffers."

Feel the Bern!

While I'm at it, let's not leave out the main attraction: guess who? Donald Trump is known for a certain complex set of standards, such as going after Obama's birth certificate for years, questioning the then-sitting president's citizenship. Trump had to know the issue was a red herring, but it got him the notoriety and exposure with the far right that became the springboard for his successful campaign. But now the chickens have come home to roost, as his political opponents are badgering the current sitting president to produce his tax returns. Once again, this is a ruse because even if they get their wish (like Trump did when Obama eventually made his birth certificate public), it won't lead to anything, other than to create doubt in people's minds.

I'm one of those people — I have a vested interest. A while back, I sold two billboards on Philadelphia bridges to Trump Plaza, a gambling casino in Atlantic City owned by The Donald. But before I could collect my commissions, Trump Plaza declared bankruptcy, leaving me much chagrined. A couple thousand bucks was no big deal to Trump, but it was to me. And still is.

I want my money!

Then there's Valeria Luiselli who wrote a book called *Tell Me How It Ends*, which is an indictment of our treatment of undocumented children. In her short book (about 100 pages), she tells the stories of children fleeing Central America for refuge in the United States ... land of the free and home of the brave? Not according to Ms. Luiselli. As one of the boys she writes about says, he left one shithole for another. Not exactly "Give me your tired, your poor, your huddled masses yearning to breathe free."

I read her book because I wanted to learn more about the kids crossing our southern border, and I think she did a very good job describing the horrible conditions they're fleeing and the challenges they face in trying to stay in the U.S. It's a tragic situation, and it certainly opened my eyes to something most people know little about (primarily because the story doesn't fit nicely into sound bites for the 6 o'clock news). I give her a lot of credit for taking a proactive approach to helping these kids, and I recommend her book.

However, while writing in great detail about the difficulties in gaining residence in the United States for the children and for herself and her family, I'm left with one question: Why? I understand why the children want to come here — they could be raped, murdered or forced to join gangs if they stayed, but why is Luiselli here? A native Mexican, she doesn't have a single positive word to say about the U.S. *Au contraire*, she is extremely critical of "Oh, beautiful for spacious skies." She brings up slavery and our treatment of Native Americans while conveniently not mentioning her homeland's treatment of its Native Mexicans. She writes about the Texas Revolution like it was a one-sided issue completely perpetrated by an aggressive, land-hungry U.S.A., while defending Mexico. She doesn't bother with bothersome details such as how badly the Mexican government was treating Texas at the time, or that it sold much of its territory to the U.S.

She was about as one-sided as can be, and even though she never articulated it, I'm guessing she likes it here because she has the right to openly bitch about the government, which she takes full advantage of. Let's face it, it's who we are: a bitchin' bunch of bitchers. We're really good at it; it's our unofficial national pastime.

Bitch, bitch, bitch!

Just stop your crying it's a sign of the times. Welcome to the final show. Hope you're wearing your best clothes.

But there are also some other things she might have pointed out that make the U.S.A. such a hot destination, like:

1. America is big, beautiful and bountiful.
2. America represents opportunity.
3. Americans are basically friendly.
4. We give away lots of free stuff.
5. We have pineapple pizza.

What more could you ask for? Maybe a little less hypocrisy.

The world can be a nasty bag of snakes, so to help you do your part in making it a healthier, safer place, I've assembled a short list of tips:

1. What goes around comes around. So when you do something nice for somebody, remember to duck.
2. If you agree 100 percent with everything someone else says, one of you is not thinking. Chances are you're both not thinking, but one of you for sure.
3. I never learned anything from people who agreed with me, other than they're obviously brilliant.
4. Good times support you, bad times strengthen you and wasted time is not wasted if you enjoy wasting time (with apologies to Bertrand Russell).
5. There are no free lunches, even if your wife makes it for you. She'll expect you to talk to her while you eat it.
6. If it's a penny for your thoughts and you put in your two cents' worth, then someone, somewhere is making a penny. (Okay, I stole that one from Steven Wright.)
7. Acts of kindness and respect trump the words kindness and respect, unless you're elected president and then ... (Oh, this one's too easy.)
8. Treat people the way you like to be treated, unless you prefer to be treated like crap. In that case, move to New York City.

9. A rolling stone gathers no moss, unless you're Keith Richards. (No joke here — just wanted to mention Keith Richards one more time.)
10. And finally, John Donne wrote:

> *No man is an island entire of itself; every man*
> *is a piece of the continent, a part of the main;*
> *if a clod be washed away by the sea, Europe*
> *is the less, as well as if a promontory were, as*
> *well as any manner of thy friends or of thine*
> *own were; any man's death diminishes me,*
> *because I am involved in mankind.*
> *And therefore, never send to know for whom*
> *the bell tolls; it tolls for thee.*

The bell tolled 31 times this past weekend, and every one of those tolls diminished *We the People*, as *We the People* run to Pilates or tee it up on the first hole. Look, I know our lives shouldn't stop with each tragedy, but can we at least take a beat to mourn and comfort each other instead of sublimating our fear into hatred? We're all in this together, remember? And the sooner we learn to engage fully in the world we live in and take responsibility for it, the better off we'll all be. John Donne's observation is a wise message to help you through your travels — and while you're on your way, here are two more thoughts I'd like you to take along: Do not surrender self for a spurious sense of safety, and remember what George Eliot said: "It's never too late to be what you might have been." In other words, keep fighting the good fight and become the best "you" you can be. That will make the world a better place.

So, until we meet again, my friends: Happy trails to you.

37

Acknowledgements

Here we are, fellow pilgrims, at my favorite part of the book: The de-acknowledgement. It's my favorite part of the book because I get the opportunity to share with you one of the fine folks who thought I was much better suited for carpentry and plumbing. Today we're here to honor Dr. Fred Johnson, one of my creative writing teachers at Rutgers. (This is going to be a long one — and a little bit sad — so you might want to grab yourself a beer and some salted nuts, or perhaps a glass of wine and a Valium ... maybe a box of tissues.)

One of the courses I took with Fred was Poetry Writing, and this is a poem I submitted in that class:

The Barber Pole

the barber pole
forever spinning up and down
never going anywhere
but always moving
has seen me pass by many times ...
and I remember
when the old men talked of Ernie Banks
but now it's all razor cuts and hair spray
... the barber pole doesn't even notice
to him I'm just another head

Besides anthropomorphizing the barber pole, *and though I'm nobody's poet, I thought it wasn't half bad* — very e e cummings with a bit of T.S. Eliot's "in the room the women come and go, talking of Michelangelo" flavor. My classmates did not agree. As a matter of fact, they hated it, and it caused some of them to achieve a proboscis improbability: wrinkling their noses and looking down them at the same time. They didn't see the palpable frustration of mankind's futile efforts to move while being stuck in the same place, or the bitter pathos of alienation in a changing world. But what seemed to bother them the most was my use of the word "head."

You see, in the 1960s and 1970s, hippies were often referred to as heads because of, you know, feeding their heads (like the Dormouse said), and most of us in those days considered ourselves hippies. It was a cute *double entendre* cleverly placed to solicit a small smile at the conclusion of this thrifty, shifty, nifty ditty. Unfortunately, I was the only one who seemed to get it, and I was told it was rather simplistic and below my normal standards, or something along those lines.

I didn't even know I had normal standards, or any standards at all, for that matter.

Nobody in class, including Fred, saw the simplistic beauty of this masterful work of art; the poignant gentleness and pulsating brilliance of saying so much with so little. They didn't get the moving experience, the sensory overload from such an uncomplicated, ordinary image.

But you see it, don't you? I mean, the power and genius are obvious, right?

Okay then.

Meanwhile, the rest of the class was submitting overwrought, emotionally linked but thematically defective cantos about the pain of being, complete with an assortment of esoteric references and opaque allusions. I didn't get a lot of that stuff; I found them deliberately arcane and self-absorbed, like most of the things you read in The New Yorker.

All through the day, I me mine, I me mine, I me mine. All through the night, I me mine, I me mine, I me mine.

I was mired in a miasma of dull, doltish, drab, dreary dreck!

What was I to do?

I sat down and wrote a new poem to express my utter befuddlement and irritation, of course:

OF HEPTIC SCEPTICS

THE INDEVIDABLE DULIPTIC
  OF CRYTIC SCRIPTIC
    INRELISHED IN PURPLE
      MURPLE SLURPLE
        FORETAILS OF THE WHORWEN
          AND THE PRICDIC ORDAN
            BUT NEVER REPLATES
              OF THE TERRBLE FATE

OF THE SCRUPTULOUS SCRUM
  WITH THE GLORDONIOUOS HUM

  WHO OUGHT HEPTICPLEX
    AN UNNUMERING HEX
      ON THE CHASED INTRAFINE
        THAT WAS LEFT FAR BEHIND
IN THE SHRIM OF THE SHRINE
THAT WAS ONE OF A KIND
AND YET PHORNOPHERS

  NOT A WORD CAN BE HEARD

OMG! You might have thought I chopped off a couple of Max Yasgur's fingers or something. And I didn't even know I was shouting back then. If they hated *The Barber Pole*, *Of Heptic Sceptics* sent them into an apoplectic rage. They were flagrantly flabbergasted.

Fred asked, "What is this?"

"It's a poem." I said.

"Are you sure?" one of the galactically stupid asked.

"Ha, ha, ha," all around.

"It doesn't say anything," Fred said.

"Exactly," I retorted.

"Were you trying to imply something here?" Fred asked.

"Exactly," I retorted again.

"But it sounds like nonsense," Fred said.

"Exactly," I re-retorted.

"Who's on first?" Fred retorted back.

And so, it was back to the drawing board for yet another attempt to send my peers into catatonic shock. This is what I came up with:

A POEM

I built a poem
of molded steel
of shining nuts & bolts
of chromated strips
of fasteners & rivets
of screws & nails & spikes
of cold iron braces
and aluminum laces

I made a poem in my driveway
amongst the cinders & gravel
and I didn't know what to make of it
it stood so erect
all sparkling clean
and I didn't know what to do with it
so I brought Fred over from next door
and asked him what did he make of it

Fred took a bite and chewed it around
and smelled and sniffed all around
and felt all around
and broke off a piece

that he put in his ear
and said that it's nice alright
all that it needs is some tightening up

So I got out my wrench and pliers
My screwdriver, my hammer and my variable-speed drill
And went to work tightening it up
Till I thought it was pretty tight
Then Fred came back and circumnavigated
The shining structure with his scrutinizing eyes
He grunted and groaned
But it would not budge
And he said, "It's much too tight"

So I got out my tools
And all l o o s e n e d it up
And stood back and watched
As it sagged & wobbled
I pushed
it around
to the front yard
and went inside to eat my lunch
trying to forget

meanwhile (as I was eating lunch)
Fred looked out of his picture window
and saw my new poem in the yard
and thought it disgraceful
and awfully hateful
and came over and took it
piece
by
shiny
piece
apart

and
stacked all
the pieces in
a bright shiny
pile in front of
my front door (and
now i go in through the
back) and no one can ever
pass by anymore without stopping
to stare at the rusty old pile as i look
out the window and smile and after careful
inspection and little reflection they ask simply
well what is it and i reply it was at one time an erection
and they say i feel it i see what you mean i know what you
mean i think thank you i say it was very very hard and they
ooouu and aaahh as they go on their way

Bingo! I hit the trifecta.

A shot of hate all around, barkeep.

I think my classmates were insulted and alarmed, not just by the apparent dis, but because Fred actually smiled when I read it, a rare occurrence that immediately separated me from the rest of the less-than-thundering herd. Even though the group never came to recognize my manifest destiny to become the next Dylan Thomas, we reached an understanding — an understanding that I was not one of them.

Fred was a rather reserved, laconic man, so when he one day indirectly implied in the most vague terms in an offhanded remark that I may have a gift, it *really blew my mind, the fact that me, an overfed long-haired leaping gnome* could cause a man with a doctorate, who taught people how to effectively communicate, to be so bad at communicating.

And it would get worse.

It's the end of my senior year and I've already secured High Honors and been inducted into Athenaeum, Rutgers Camden's honor society, but the big prize was the writing award, an honor I coveted greatly. It was assumed by people in the know (mainly me and other intelligent, insightful individuals) that I would win the award.

So I'm feeling pretty good as I'm walking across campus a few days before graduation when a young lady (who shall remain nameless because I can't remember how to spell her name), comes bursting out of the Student Center waving her hands and yelling at me, "I won the award, Richard, I won the writing award."

I was stunned. I couldn't move and could hardly speak. It reminded me of a time when I was about 10 years old and a girl in my class came down the street sitting crossed-legged in the open back of a brand-new station wagon, waving her hands and yelling at me, "Look, Richard, my daddy's new car!" And it was a beaut: big and shiny and loaded to the gills as I stood there next to the old, beat-up junker that my mom could afford, dazed and expressionless, just like with my nameless classmate, smiling and waving and yelling and jumping around and expecting me to be excited for her.

I think I managed a congratulations and dispassionate hug, but I was totally numb, in total disbelief, a total wreck.

A few minutes later I'm standing in Fred's office and he's avoiding eye contact, looking guilty because we'd talked about the award and it was my impression I was in like Flint. "You deserved the award," Fred finally said, looking up at me as he sat at his desk, nervously fumbling with a pen. "But it will do her more good; it will help her a great deal more than it would help you. You don't need it." And with those few words I was transported back to Camp Ockanickon, or, as the great un-articulator, Yogi Berra, would have put it, "It was déjà vu all over again."

Camp Ockanickon gave out different-colored feathers in a campfire ceremony at the end of each two-week session. I attended the camp for many years and stayed the entire summer, all eight weeks, which meant I had four shots a year at the feathers I wanted most: the white one and the blue one. The white feather was awarded to the best camper in a village, the highest honor at the dramatic ceremony, complete with tom-toms, chants, ornately feathered headdresses and American Indian garb (a pretty cool event where we were taught a lot about Indian lore and culture). A village was made up of several cabins, and each cabin had six campers and a counselor. This may come as a shock to you, but I was a fairly obnoxious kid, so getting the white feather was out of the question, especially because the same counselors I deliberately antagonized voted on it.

I would have loved to have won a white feather, but I was a realist. However, the blue feather — awarded to a camper in each cabin and voted on by his bunkmates — was a possibility. I worked at it, but as I mentioned, I could be somewhat insufferable, not to mention overly competitive in an extremely competitive environment, so there was the hate factor, too. Accordingly, much like the white feather, I began to believe it was an impossibility.

That said, during the last session of my last summer, I made up my mind to win the blue feather. I tried to ingratiate myself to my bunkmates; I was benevolent and obsequious to the point where I could barely stand myself, and to be perfectly frank, I thought I nailed it. So you can imagine my disappointment when the vote resulted in a three-three tie between me and some kid who swallowed worms whole to the delight of the other campers. Our counselor conducted three more votes, and each one ended in a tie, so he decided he would cast the deciding vote.

All right. The big night. Lots of tom-tom playing and tribal dancing and whooping it up and I was superciliously confident — how could our counselor, a wise man of 18, vote for a guy who swallows worms? So when the worm-swallower's name was called instead of mine, I was crushed. I remember standing in front of our counselor later that night, just like standing in front of Fred, and being told that the feather would do the worm-swallower more good than it would me, that I was awarded every activity feather available, seven altogether, including the much-sought-after yellow feather for being the best fighter in our once-a-session, all-day Indian games (which was really just flag wrestling).

Our counselor told me that old worm-swallower only got one activity feather and I had so many, and besides, he concluded, "You don't need it."

Wow! Here it was many years later in Fred's office and I still don't need it.

Well, I have some news for you guys: I NEEDED THAT DAMN BLUE FEATHER AND I NEEDED THAT DAMN WRITING AWARD!

I hope that clears that up.

And while we're on the subject of de-acknowledgement, take my wife ...

... Terry. You thought I was going to write "please," didn't you? but I would never disrespect her like that. She's always my first reader and puts up with my disappearing into *a clean, well-lighted place* for days on end, but inexplicably, she doesn't get my poetry — she would have been a perfect fit for Fred's poetry writing class. Keep in mind, she went to Penn State, where she majored in football games and fraternity parties, and once told me that she doesn't like opera because it sounds like they're singing in a foreign language. Respectfully submitted.

(I'm dead!)

In acknowledgement (quickly), I'd like to begin with Dina Hall, the talented artist who designed the covers of all three of my books. I've been working with Dina for more than 30 years, and who knew way back then what a talented shooting star with a guitar she'd become? Check her out.

Speaking of stars, Terree O'Neill Yeagle of The Moment Photography is a star with a camera and has done her best to make me look good through several configurations of my ever-transitioning face.

As always, I need to thank my friend John Hayes. He's been

a valuable advisor, and you know, it's funny, but the more he likes my writing, the more I like him. Go figure.

Bill Kline has been editing my columns for years and has loaned his keen eye and professional direction to this manuscript. He's one of the good guys!

Kerry Boderman, the queen of punctuation, has diligently worked on all three of my books, offering germane and perceptive suggestions. Anything she touches gets better.

Finally, there's Brenda Lange, who's been with me for the entire journey. She is my editor, my biggest supporter, my spiritual savior and my literary guardian who keeps me from going off the tracks. If you like my stuff, thank Brenda.

38

Bibliography of Unattributed Quotations

Introduction

A screaming comes across the sky — Thomas Pynchon, *Gravity's Rainbow*

... time's winged chariot hurrying near — Andrew Marvell, *To His Coy Mistress*

Though nothing can bring back the hour, etc. — William Wordsworth, *Ode to Intimations of Immortality from Recollections of Early Childhood*

... long and winding road — John Lennon and Paul McCartney, *The Long and Winding Road*

Prologue

Nice work if you can get it, etc. — George and Ira Gershwin, *Nice Work if You Can Get It*

I want to get drunk, etc. — Rudy Toombs, *One Scotch, One Bourbon, One Beer*

... a first-class tragic trauma — John Barth, *Giles Goat Boy*

... and never the twain shall meet — Rudyard Kipling, *The Ballad of East and West*

... talk is cheap when the story is good, etc. — Gary Dean Richrath, *Take It on the Run*

In my little town, etc. — Paul Simon, *My Little Town*

... were glowing like a metal, etc. — Jim Steinman, *Paradise by the Dashboard Lights*

This above all, etc. — William Shakespeare, *Hamlet*

Marching Onward

... we few, we happy few — William Shakespeare, *Henry V*

Relax, Nothing is Under Control
... a constant battle for the ultimate state of control — Billy Joel, *A Matter of Trust*

Vote for Me, I'll Set You Free
If there are four guys, and you're Ringo — *Jersey Boys*

Everywhere There's Lots of Piggies — George Harrison, *Piggies*
... crawling in the dirt — George Harrison, *Piggies*
... in their starched white shirts — George Harrison, *Piggies*

Don't Be a George, Part 1
Holy Father, what's the matter? etc. — Eric Bazilian and Rob Hyman, *All you Zombies*
You don't have to hide anymore! — Eric Bazilian and Rob Hyman, *All you Zombies*

Don't Be a George, Part 3
... mouth alive with juices like wine — Duran Duran, *Hungry Like the Wolf*

Ch-ch-ch-ch-changes (turn and face the strange) — David Bowie, *Changes*

White Noise
that's the way, uh-huh, etc. — Richard Finch and Harry Wayne Casey, *That's the Way (I Like It)*
... busy doing something close to nothing — Prince, *Raspberry Beret*
... this is what it sounds like when doves cry — Prince, *When Doves Cry*

Sailboats in the Desert
One two three, etc. — Leonard Borisoff, David White and John Madara, *1-2-3*

Rhinoceros? Imposerous!
We got move these refrigerators, etc. — Mark Knopfler, *Money for Nothing*

Who's the Boss?
All the lonely people, etc. — John Lennon and Paul McCartney, *Eleanor Rigby*

I'm Late, I'm Late, for a Very Important Date — Lewis Carroll, *Alice's Adventures in Wonderland*
I had a brother at Khe Sanh, etc. — Bruce Springsteen, *Born in the U.S.A.*
When logic and proportion, etc. — Grace Slick, *White Rabbit*

All the Wrong Junk in All the Wrong Places
Future's so bright, etc. — Pat MacDonald, *The Future's so Bright*

Of Profiles, Roles and Pigeonholes, Part 1
... a man of wealth and taste — Mick Jagger and Keith Richards, *Sympathy for the Devil*
... faces come out of the rain and *no one remembers your name* — Robby Krieger and Jim Morrison, *People are Strange*

Of Profiles, Roles and Pigeonholes, Part 2
... time flies over us, etc. — Nathanial Hawthorne, *The Marble Faun*
... every breath you take, etc. and *... every move you make,* etc. — Gordon Sumner, *Every Breath you Take*

Of Profiles, Roles and Pigeonholes, Part 3
... do this, don't do that, etc. — Les Emmerson, *Signs*

Of Profiles, Roles and Pigeonholes, Conclusion
You think I'm a whore, etc. — David Johansen, *Heart of Gold*

... throw that speedball by you, etc. — Bruce Springsteen, *Glory Days*

Pack up the babies, etc. — Neil Diamond, *Brother Love's Traveling Salvation Show*

We few, we happy few, etc. — Ibid-ish

... Jumpin' Jack Flash — Mick Jagger and Keith Richards, *Jumpin' Jack Flash*

... set up, like a bowlin' pin, etc. — Jerry Garcia, Phil Lesh, Bob Weir and Robert Hunter, *Truckin'*

... nobody calls me sir. You got the wrong guy, etc. — *The Big Lebowski*

and speaking of getting old ...

... and dying to me don't sound, etc. — John Mellencamp, *The Authority Song*

The Dog Kicker, et al.

the beauty, the splendor, etc. — Gerome Ragni, James Rado and Galt MacDermot, *Hair*

Adjustment Bureau

Changes in latitudes, changes in attitudes, etc. — Jimmy Buffett, *Changes in Latitudes, Changes in Attitudes*

Unsocial Media

Abandon all hope, etc. — Dante Alighieri, *Inferno*

... in the autumn mist in a land called Honah Lee — Peter Yarrow and Leonard Lipton, *Puff the Magic Dragon*

To Serve Man

Don't wanna be an American idiot, — Billie Joe Armstrong, Tre Cool and Mike Dirnt, *American Idiot*

You dad gum guv'ment, etc. — Roger Miller, *Guv'ment*

... cause fire is the devil's only friend — Don McLean, *American Pie*

... *to take arms against a sea of troubles,* etc. — William Shakespeare, *Hamlet*

Here I come to save the day — Terrytooes, *Mighty Mouse*

It don't come easy; etc. — Ringo Starr, *It Don't Come Easy*

Welcome my son, welcome to the machine, etc. — Roger Waters, *Welcome to the Machine*

We need a movement with a quickness, etc. — Zack de la Rocha, *Take the Power Back*

... *rage, rage against the dying of the light and do not go gentle into that good night* — Dylan Thomas, *Do Not Go Gently into that Good Night*

You are a fluke of the universe, etc. — Tony Hendra, *Deteriorata*

The bitch is back — Bernie Taupin and Elton John, *The Bitch is Back*

Throw 'em a fake and a finagle, etc. — Fred Ebb and John Kander, *Razzle Dazzle*

You're my end and my beginning, etc. — John Legend and Toby Gad, *All of Me*

I am I cried, I am said I — Neil Diamond, *I Am ... I Said*

Sloppy Sue and Big Bone Billy — Bruce Springsteen, *Rosalita*

Get over it, get over it, etc. — Glenn Frey and Don Henley, *Get Over It*

Whether you think you can, etc. — Henry Ford

Got to pull myself together, etc. — Kim Carnes, *Crazy in the Night*

... *and when you get the choice to sit it out,* etc. — Tia Sellers and Mark Sanders, *I Hope you Dance*

To Be or Not to Be, That is the Question — William Shakespeare, *Hamlet*

Goodbye cruel world, I'm off to join the circus — Gloria Shayne, *Goodbye Cruel World*

Total Eclipse of the Brain

Oh, but Mama, that's where the fun is — Bruce Springsteen, *Blinded by the Light*

I just want something to hold on to, etc. — Bruce Springsteen, *Human Touch*

Epilogue

You can bury your dead, but don't leave a trace, etc. — P.F. Sloan, *Eve of Destruction*

You and I must make a pact. We must bring salvation back. — Berry Gordy Jr., Bob West, Hal Davis and Willie Hutch, *I'll Be There*

Just stop your crying it's a sign of the times, etc. — Harry Styles, Alex Salibian, Jeffrey Bhasker, Mitchell Rowland, Ryan Nasci and Tyler Johnson, *Sign of the Times*

Acknowledgements

... and though I'm nobody's poet, etc. — Rupert Holmes, *Escape (The Piña Colada Song)*

All through the day, I me mine, etc. — George Harrison, *I Me Mine*

... really blew my mind, the fact that me, etc. — Charles Miller, Harold Brown, Howard Scott, Lee Levitin, Lonnie Jordan, B.B. Dickerson and Papa Dee Allen, *Spill the Wine*

... clean, well-lighted place — Ernest Hemingway, *A Clean Well-Lighted Place*